THE EVERYTHING

EASY LARGE-PRINT
CROSSWORDS BOOK

VOLUME 9

Dear Reader,

These crossword puzzles are easy enough to be solvable yet challenging enough to keep you thinking. I think it is a nice balance. For physical exercise, you don't need to run marathons or climb mountains to stay healthy. For mental exercise, solving these puzzles is comparable to taking a brisk walk in the park. It's a fun and rewarding experience! Beginners, and those who have been frustrated with more difficult crossword puzzles, are welcome here.

For me, this kind of mental exercise is a wonderful way to relax. Losing yourself in a crossword puzzle can be a nice diversion from the hubbub of life. Easy puzzles are better because being stumped with harder puzzles is *not* relaxing!

To make things even more pleasant, these puzzles are large. It's easy to read the clues, and easy to write the answers into the puzzle grids. I hope you enjoy solving these crossword puzzles as much as I enjoyed creating them!

Welcome to the EVERYTHING® Series!

These handy, accessible books give you all you need to tackle a difficult project, gain a new hobby, comprehend a fascinating topic, prepare for an exam, or even brush up on something you learned back in school but have since forgotten.

You can choose to read an Everything® book from cover to cover or just pick out the information you want from our four useful boxes: e-questions, e-facts, e-alerts, and e-ssentials. We give you everything you need to know on the subject, but throw in a lot of fun stuff along the way too.

We now have more than 400 Everything® books in print, spanning such wide-ranging categories as weddings, pregnancy, cooking, music instruction, foreign language, crafts, pets, New Age, and so much more. When you're done reading them all, you can finally say you know Everything®!

PUBLISHER Karen Cooper

MANAGING EDITOR, EVERYTHING® SERIES Lisa Laing

COPY CHIEF Casey Ebert

PRODUCTION EDITOR Jo-Anne Duhamel

ACQUISITIONS EDITOR Lisa Laing

EVERYTHING® SERIES COVER DESIGNER Erin Alexander

Visit the entire Everything® series at www.everything.com

THE EVERYTHING EASY LARGE-PRINT CROSSWORDS BOOK

VOLUME 9

More than 120 fun and easy
puzzles in large print

Charles Timmerman
Founder of Funster.com

Adams Media
New York London Toronto Sydney New Delhi

Dedicated to Suzanne, Calla, and Meryl.

Adams Media
An Imprint of Simon & Schuster, Inc.
100 Technology Center Drive
Stoughton, MA 02072

An Everything® Series Book.

Everything® and everything.com® are registered trademarks of Simon & Schuster, Inc.

First Adams Media trade paperback edition March 2022

ADAMS MEDIA and colophon are trademarks of Simon & Schuster.

For information about special discounts for bulk purchases, please contact Simon & Schuster Special Sales at 1-866-506-1949 or business@simonandschuster.com.

The Simon & Schuster Speakers Bureau can bring authors to your live event. For more information or to book an event contact the Simon & Schuster Speakers Bureau at 1-866-248-3049 or visit our website at www.simonspeakers.com.

Manufactured in the United States of America

10 9 8 7 6 5

ISBN 978-1-5072-1914-0

Acknowledgments

I would like to thank each and every one of the more than half million people who have visited my website, Funster.com, to play word games and puzzles. You have shown me how much fun puzzles can be and how addictive they can become!

It is a pleasure to acknowledge the folks at Adams Media who made this book possible. I particularly want to thank my editor, Lisa Laing, for so skillfully managing the many projects we have worked on together.

Contents

Introduction / 8

Puzzles / 11

Answers / 257

Introduction

What do Rosa Parks, Richard Nixon, Jesse Owens, and crossword puzzles have in common? They were all born in the year 1913. In that year, a journalist named Arthur Wynne published a "word-cross" puzzle in the *New York World*'s Sunday newspaper. Though it was diamond-shaped, it had all of the features of the crossword puzzles that we know and love today. The name evolved into *crossword* as the paper continued to publish the popular word puzzles.

It wasn't until 1924 that the first book of crossword puzzles was published. That was when the crossword craze really began. It joined other fads of the Roaring Twenties like goldfish swallowing, flagpole sitting, yo-yos, and pogo sticks. Of course, not all of these fads survived (perhaps fortunately).

Besides crossword puzzles, some really beautiful things came out of the 1920s. In music, jazz surged in popularity and George Gershwin's *Rhapsody in Blue* was performed for the first time. In literature, F. Scott Fitzgerald published some of his most enduring novels, including *The Great Gatsby*. In design, it was the beginning of art deco. That's how the world was shifting when crossword puzzles came of age.

Crossword puzzles became popular closer to a time when entertainment required *active* participation. In those days, people actually played sports rather than watched them, told each other stories rather than turned on the TV, and even sang songs rather than streamed them. Like entertainment of yesteryear, crossword puzzles require your active participation. And this is a refreshing change for those of us who still enjoy a mental workout.

Today, nearly every major newspaper runs a crossword puzzle. Entire sections of bookstores are devoted to crossword puzzle books. (Thanks for choosing this one!) Indeed, crosswords are probably the most common word puzzle in the world.

Why do crossword puzzles continue to be so popular? Only you can answer that question since there are as many reasons to work a crossword puzzle as there are solvers. But perhaps it has something to do with the convenient marriage of fun and learning that crossword puzzles offer.

Puzzles

ACROSS

1. Pouches
5. Catch red-handed
8. Tex-___ cuisine
11. Salt Lake City's state
12. Children's head pests
13. PC maker
14. Emulate Greg Louganis
15. Numbered musical work
16. CEO's degree
17. *A Streetcar Named Desire* woman
19. Negligent
21. God-given
23. Dashboard abbr.
26. Last of 26
27. Sleeves cover them
31. Previously owned
33. Headbutt
35. Flintstones' pet
36. Selfish one's exclamation
37. Stranded motorist's need
39. Violist's need
40. "Michael, Row Your Boat ___"
43. Right away
46. Curious thing
51. Mouse sighter's cry
52. Holds the title to
54. Muskogee native
55. *All Things Considered* airer
56. Will-___-wisp
57. Ten: prefix
58. One ___ customer
59. Response to an online joke
60. Sturdy trees

DOWN

1. Lather
2. Hard ___ (toiling away)
3. Stalagmite site
4. Author Silverstein
5. Bite like a pup
6. Lexus competitor
7. Assailed on all sides
8. Actress Rogers who was once married to Tom Cruise
9. ___ and flows
10. "Do not open 'til ___"
12. Temporary wheels
18. Actress Taylor, familiarly
20. Hoover Dam's lake
22. Nifty, in the '50s
23. "The word," to secret keepers
24. Letter before omega
25. Farm brooder
28. Tease
29. Six, on a phone dial
30. "You reap what you ___"
32. College faculty head
34. Moody
38. Joined in matrimony

41. Pub perch

42. Do-it-yourselfer's book genre

43. ___-up rage

44. Seized vehicle

45. Cajun cuisine vegetable

47. Birdbrain

48. Swedish furniture retailer

49. Lyme disease transmitter

50. Nays' opposites

53. Stanley Cup grp.

Solution on Page 258

ACROSS

1. Like monsoon season
4. Machine tooth
7. Uppermost point
11. Kitchen gadget brand
12. Brit of FOX News
14. "I double ___ you!"
15. Civil ___
16. Memo-heading abbr.
17. Belonging to us
18. Mrs. Eisenhower
20. Little women
22. Watchdog's warning
23. "___ changed my mind"
24. Hat's edge
27. Genetic info carrier
28. Nav. system
31. Water closet, informally
32. Luster
34. Mai ___ (rum-based beverage)
35. "___ will be done"
36. The Say ___ Kid (Willie Mays)
37. Prom dress
38. Actor Linden or Holbrook
39. Toilet paper layer
41. Point the finger at
43. Furniture polish scent
46. Heroic deed
47. Sports org. with a March tourney
49. London forecast
51. 5K, e.g.
52. As neat as ___
53. *Alice* spinoff
54. Annoys
55. Map lines: abbr.
56. Grass in strips

DOWN

1. "Holy cow!"
2. Word with eye or final
3. Synagogue scroll
4. Committee head
5. ___ Mongolia
6. All clocks are set by it: abbr.
7. Love like crazy
8. Legendary Bunyan
9. Makes a misstep
10. Crosses (out)
13. Wankel or diesel
19. Grand Hotel studio
21. As a czar, he was terrible
24. Sandwich served with a toothpick
25. Shout from the bleachers
26. Campus climber
27. Actress Susan
28. Classic muscle car
29. Cat's foot
30. Envy or lust
32. Sam the ___ and the Pharaohs
33. Montana's capital

37. Workout facility

38. Despises

39. Tartan pattern

40. ___ on (pressures)

41. Yogi or Smokey

42. Be deficient in

44. Kills, in mob slang

45. ___ contendere (court plea)

46. "Casual" dress day: abbr.

48. EMS procedure

50. "In ___ We Trust"

Solution on Page 258

ACROSS

1. Phoenix's home: abbr.
5. Pay or Cray ending
8. Pond scum component
12. Choice for Hamlet
13. Nat. that underwent reunification
14. Laid eyes on
15. Guy known for his "Auld Lang Syne" rendition
17. Four-footed friends
18. Highway: abbr.
19. Wire service
21. Diarist Nin
23. Shoulder bag feature
26. Have faith in
27. Removes
29. Suffix with hotel
30. Distress signal at sea
31. Church bench
32. Goofs
35. Hunger for
37. Renter's document
38. Prior to, old-style
39. Air blower
40. Hip, in the '60s
41. Winter Olympics sled
44. Liquidation sale
49. Burden
50. German "a"
51. Yes-___ question
52. Admin. aide
53. Gas pump choice: abbr.
54. Pass over

DOWN

1. City in GA
2. "Winnie-the-Pooh" baby
3. "Think" sloganeer
4. Striped equines
5. Fairy tale monsters
6. Was out in front
7. Wakens
8. Strive
9. Gen. Robert E. ___
10. ___-up-and-go
11. Opposite of a ques.
16. "While you're ___…"
20. Jim and Tammy's old club
21. Spinning dizzily
22. Nightingale or Barton, e.g.
24. Even, on the leaderboard
25. "Pet" annoyance
26. QB Tebow
27. Uno, ___, tres
28. Stockholm's land: abbr.
30. Actor Tracy
33. Least perilous
34. Land between Can. and Mex.
35. Corp. money managers
36. Cowboy contests

38. "You're ___ friends"

41. Hawaii's Mauna ___

42. Young ___ (tots)

43. Astronaut Grissom

45. Tell a fib

46. Mork's home planet

47. Single: prefix

48. "On ___ of Old Smokey"

Solution on Page 258

ACROSS

1. Med school grad
4. Steep, as tea
8. Pond gunk
12. Ore-___ (frozen food brand)
13. Babe with a bat
14. "I get it," humorously
15. "___ Dieu!"
16. Wrong
18. Wipe, as a blackboard
20. Alexander of the Reagan cabinet
21. "What's the ___?" ("Who cares?")
22. Puts in the mail
26. Just ___ (very little)
28. Rouse from slumber
31. "___ so sorry!"
32. Deity
33. Painful spots
34. Day-___ paint
35. Inner tube filler
36. Dawdling
37. Tory's opponent
38. More cunning
40. Campsite bed
41. Turn over a new ___
44. Story-telling uncle
47. State between Texas and Arizona:
   2 wds.
51. *The Simpsons* clerk
52. Butter look-alike
53. Tanguay and Gabor
54. Edge of a canyon
55. Lobster eaters' wear
56. Does needlework
57. Mind reader's ability

DOWN

1. Five-and-___
2. Olfactory stimulation
3. Ginger ale brand
4. Short
5. Campaign (for)
6. Make an engraving
7. "Hold it right there!"
8. Beetle Bailey's boss
9. Cuban hero Guevara
10. L.A. school
11. Bon ___ (witty saying)
17. Greets the day
19. Caesar of comedy
23. Bad dream
24. Artist Salvador
25. Unhealthy air
26. "What ___!" ("Such fun!")
27. Work hard
28. Apt rhyme for *pursue*
29. Noah's ship
30. Lock opener
33. Buying binge
37. Sorrow

39. St. ____ fire

40. Annoyed

42. Chopping tools

43. Quitting time, for some

45. "Breaking ____ Hard to Do"

46. ____ pump (drainage aid)

47. San Francisco's ____ Hill

48. Pharmaceutical giant ____ Lilly

49. Spider's creation

50. Crow sound

Solution on Page 258

ACROSS

1. Miss Garbo
6. Dentist's deg.
9. And so forth, for short
12. Deprive of weapons
13. ___-Man (arcade game)
14. Chat room guffaw
15. Auto racer Andretti
16. Dream up
18. Geeky one
20. Printed mistakes
21. ___ Palace
24. Religious doctrine
25. B&B beverages
26. Knights' weapons
28. King Cole and Turner
30. Cow call
31. Excellent, in modern slang
35. Emotional shock
38. Each and every one
39. Saturate (with)
42. Ill-fated liner
44. Wee
46. Corn throwaways
47. ___ break (TV intermission)
49. Weaving machines
52. City reg.
53. Music with jazzlike riffs
54. Light purple
55. Flattens in the ring, for short
56. Disabled vehicle's need
57. Laziness

DOWN

1. Wrigley's product
2. Some genetic coding, for short
3. Heartfelt
4. Attempts
5. Without principles
6. Printer resolution meas.
7. Knight's lady
8. Hard to find
9. Cuban boat boy Gonzalez
10. Kemo Sabe's companion
11. Spotless
17. Take hold of
19. Theater school study
21. Chili ___ carne
22. Double-platinum Steely Dan album
23. Animal nose
27. Stand-up performer
29. Daredevil's feat
32. Harrison Ford's Star Wars role
33. "___ Baba and the Forty Thieves"
34. Special attention, for short
36. Stand up to
37. Coral rings
39. Consoling phrase
40. ___-Goldwyn-Mayer
41. Necklace components

43. Bubbling on the stove

45. ___ Ono

48. No, slangily

50. Doorstep welcomer

51. High or elementary: abbr.

Solution on Page 259

ACROSS

1. Cry of anticipation
5. Bit of hair gel
8. BBs and bullets
12. Actress Russo
13. Lincoln's nickname
14. "Beam ___, Scotty!"
15. Smile widely
16. Uno + due
17. MIT part: abbr.
18. South African golfer Ernie
19. Prefix meaning "new"
20. Admin. aides
21. Crusted dessert
23. Piercing tools
25. Chocolate alternative
27. Opus ___ (*The Da Vinci Code* group)
28. Overseer of corp. accounts
31. Park or Fifth, say
33. Place with swinging doors
35. Big: abbr.
36. Fond du ___, Wisconsin
38. They're always underfoot
39. ___ Lee (cake company)
40. A prima donna's needs stroking
41. Hindu social division
44. Air gun ammo
46. Jay-Z's genre
49. "___ can you see…"
50. Kung ___ chicken
51. Lavish party
52. Gold source
53. Advice columnist Landers
54. Garden with forbidden fruit
55. Feasts upon
56. Slip behind
57. Holiday drinks

DOWN

1. Kill ___ killed (law of the jungle)
2. Toe's opposite
3. Unrestrained
4. ___ and haw
5. July 4, 1776, e.g.
6. Like an American in Paris
7. Stinging insect
8. Not quite right
9. Restroom door word
10. Has to
11. Elects (to)
19. Interstellar clouds
20. Assumed names
22. Particle with a charge
24. *Fantastic Mr. Fox* director Anderson
25. Pres. Coolidge
26. Part of GPA: abbr.
28. Grand Canyon river
29. No friend

30. Clip-___ (certain sunglasses)

32. Either end of a wide grin

34. Ship's record

37. Beach shelter

39. Eyelid inflammations

41. "Ready or not, here I ___!"

42. Where Japan is

43. Film director Gus Van ___

45. Sound from Big Ben

47. "Break ___!" ("Good luck!")

48. Thumbs-down reviews

50. Bosom buddy

51. ___-Xers (boomers' kids)

Solution on Page 259

ACROSS

1. A/C measures
5. No longer used: abbr.
8. "…more than one way to skin ___"
12. Powerful DC lobby
13. Angkor ___ (Cambodian temple)
14. Prefix with gram or graph
15. Pickling herb
16. One-eighty from SSW
17. Withdraw gradually
18. "Doe, ___, a female…"
20. Nile nippers
21. Spoke impudently to
24. Tel Aviv's land: abbr.
26. Solemn pledges
27. The Sunshine State, briefly
28. "That's a laugh!"
31. Toy store ___ Schwarz
32. Screwed up
34. "___ tree falls…"
35. Knock lightly
36. Big outdoor gear retailer
37. Sees romantically
39. Sprint competitor
40. Fully prepared
41. Emily of etiquette
44. Thesaurus compiler
46. "___ only trying to help"
47. Lawyers' org.
48. "…hear ___ drop"
52. French film
53. Person with a beat
54. Tabula ___ (blank slate)
55. Big video game maker
56. Golf ball elevator
57. Clean the deck

DOWN

1. Rotten to the core
2. Mai ___ (rum drink)
3. Website ID
4. Daryl Hannah comedy of '84
5. Possessed
6. ___ of one's existence
7. Germ-free
8. In armed conflict
9. So-so marks
10. "Take ___!" (track coach's order)
11. Perfect gymnastics scores
19. Gobi or Mojave
21. Cushiony
22. Extremely narrow, as a shoe
23. Pull the plug on
25. Equestrian's seat
27. TGIF day
28. Chart toppers
29. For ___ (not gratis)
30. "…why ___ thou forsaken me?"
33. Take back, as a public statement
38. Sacrificial sites

39. On a cruise

40. Open-mouthed

41. Photos, briefly

42. Painful boo-boo

43. Performed an aria

45. Long, thin musical instrument

49. Furry foot

50. "…for what ___ man…"

51. Take into custody

Solution on Page 259

ACROSS

1. Baby's dinner wear
4. ___ point (never)
8. Serenade
12. "Who ___ to judge?"
13. Start of many Ocean Spray juice flavors
14. Earnest request
15. Have a gabfest
16. Daly of *Judging Amy*
17. Heart charts, for short
18. Division of a play
20. Employee protection org.
22. Put two and two together, say
24. Dental care brand
28. Small argument
31. Subsides, as the tide
34. Really small
35. Attila, for one
36. Alphas' followers
37. Ad ___ committee
38. "Anchors Aweigh" branch: abbr.
39. Ostrich cousins
40. Hit on the head
41. Bangkok natives
43. Anat. or chem.
45. Silent assents
48. It's connected to the left ventricle
52. Greek love god
55. Helps
57. Tour transportation
58. Fermented rice beverage
59. Very dry, as wine
60. It's like "-like"
61. Dermatologist's removal
62. Brothers and sisters, for short
63. "Lucy in the ___ with Diamonds"

DOWN

1. Howls at the moon
2. Apple computer
3. Two-wheeler
4. Performed on stage
5. Give it a shot
6. iPod Mini successor
7. Binary digits
8. Thrown weapon
9. Similar type
10. Opposite of pos.
11. Petrol
19. Singer ___ King Cole
21. A Ponderosa son
23. Pass judgment
25. Dr. Seuss's *Horton Hears* ___
26. Spinks or Trotsky
27. At one's ___ and call
28. Open-and-___ case
29. Shove
30. Model ___ Nicole Smith
32. A/C stat
33. Striped fish

36. "You'd ___ Nice to Come Home To"

40. Brief life story?

42. Map within a map

44. Hurls

46. Uses a powder puff

47. iPhone assistant

49. Hitting stats

50. Ivory source

51. Like a fireplace floor

52. Exit-the-program key

53. Comic actor Romano

54. Agrees to

56. Do a voice-over for

Solution on Page 259

ACROSS

1. Industrial tub
4. Russian parliament
8. Advanced degree: abbr.
11. Heart chart: abbr.
12. SASE, e.g.
13. Oxford or loafer
14. F–J connection
15. Naughty child's Christmas gift
16. Imitate
17. Get an ___ effort
19. Oz canine
21. Gave dinner
23. Mock
26. Part of EDT
30. Prickly shrub
32. Hoops org.
33. Moonshine container
35. WBA decision
36. Dentist's tool
39. Tournament favorite
42. Assumed name
44. Halen or Morrison
45. *The Art of Love* poet
47. ___ of the Unknown Soldier
50. Freshly cut, as a lawn
53. Stupefy
55. Diamond or ruby
57. "Take ___ a compliment"
58. Fifty-fifty
59. Dishcloth
60. Freud's "I"
61. Borscht vegetable
62. Addition total

DOWN

1. ___ out (relax, like, totally)
2. Reason for a backrub
3. End-of-week cry
4. Edict
5. Numero ___ (top dog)
6. Future doc's exam
7. Distribute, as shares
8. Vietnamese noodle soup
9. Go like a bunny
10. *L.A. Law* costar Susan
13. Search high and low
18. Frequently, in verse
20. File folder projection
22. Julius Erving's nickname
24. Nick at ___
25. Grab hold of
26. Final stage
27. Cadabra preceder
28. Compete for the America's Cup
29. Bolt attachment
31. Curtain hanger
34. White House URL suffix
37. Detroit footballers
38. Restroom, informally

40. Inventor's protection
41. ___-cone (frozen treat)
43. Lesser-played half of a 45
46. Letterman, to friends
48. Baseball bosses: abbr.
49. Jeff Bridges's brother
50. 1,002, in old Rome

51. Needing no prescription: abbr.
52. "Doo ___ Diddy": 1964 song
54. Letter after wye
56. *Ben-Hur* studio

Solution on Page 260

ACROSS

1. Old telecom giant
4. Beach lotion letters
7. China's ___ Xiaoping
11. Sounds of surprise
12. "If I ___ Hammer"
14. Escape route
15. Big Apple paper, initially
16. Misses the mark
17. Jay of *The Tonight Show*
18. Home furnishings chain
20. Stockholm natives
22. Tennessee senator Alexander
24. Ham or hamburger
25. Words of confidence
26. OPEC units
29. Belfry flier
30. *Inferno* writer
31. ___ Kippur
33. Fixes, as a shoe
35. Let fall
36. Wire diameter units
37. Human ___
38. Vegas attraction
41. Group that votes alike
42. Frankenstein's assistant
43. Supermodel Banks
45. It climbs the walls
48. Honky-___
49. Penn or Connery
50. Moo ___ pork (Chinese dish)
51. Breakfast choice
52. Big Apple inits.
53. "Naughty, naughty!"

DOWN

1. Suffix for shapes
2. Iron Maiden's "Hallowed Be ___ Name"
3. Pre-repair job figure
4. Transparent, as stockings
5. Prefix with graph
6. New Deal pres.
7. X out
8. Crossed (out)
9. Cloud number
10. Classic muscle cars
13. States
19. Neb. neighbor
21. Suffix with silver or glass
22. Ad-___ (improvise)
23. Rent-___ (airport service)
24. Lions' hair
26. Votes
27. Writer of song words
28. Any time now
30. "Nothin' ___!"
32. Fuel efficiency abbr.
34. Smug smiles
35. "Gloria in Excelsis ___"

37. Mont ___

38. Mention as an example

39. More than eager

40. iTunes download

41. Jackass's sound

44. Itching desire

46. Videotape format

47. Laugh syllable

Solution on Page 260

ACROSS

1. Crazy ___ loon
4. Heights: abbr.
8. Wyatt of *Tombstone*
12. Flower holder
13. Dinghy or dory
14. Love, in Latin
15. Soft touch
16. ___-inflammatory
17. Corn Belt tower
18. Lovers' rendezvous
20. ___ Peanut Butter Cups
22. Harden, as plaster
24. NBC weekend comedy, briefly
25. Middle of the ocean
29. Russian royals
33. Gym iteration
34. When the sun shines
36. Patriotic women's org.
37. Hide away
40. Baffled
43. Suffix with ball or bass
45. Beats by ___ (headphones brand)
46. Home music system
49. Endures
53. It's where the heart is
54. Lab rat's challenge
57. Have a cold, say
58. ___ and crafts
59. Have ___ (be connected)
60. Pod inhabitant
61. Basic idea
62. Shower affection (on)
63. Lose tautness

DOWN

1. PDA entry
2. Zoom up
3. Bar member: abbr.
4. Subsides
5. Creepy Chaney
6. Body art, in slang
7. Mixes
8. Painting stands
9. *Lucky Jim* author Kingsley
10. Auditioner's goal
11. Major leaguers
19. Form 1040 ID
21. Suffix with differ
23. Longtime senator Kennedy
25. Surgery sites, briefly
26. Housebroken animal
27. Emissions watchdog: abbr.
28. Motorists' grp.
30. Commotion
31. ___ Tafari (Haile Selassie)
32. Next year's alums: abbr.
35. From Jan. 1 to now
38. Most achy
39. Bladed gardening tool

41. *What's My Line?* panelist Francis
42. Meadow
44. Desert wanderer
46. Kind of carpet
47. Spelling of *Beverly Hills, 90210*
48. CPR experts
50. Maple syrup sources

51. "___ Yellow Ribbon Round the Ole Oak Tree"
52. Smelter's waste
55. "It's ___-win situation!"
56. Clearasil target, informally

Solution on Page 260

ACROSS

1. Expressed, as farewell
5. USN bigwig
8. Throw in the towel
12. Fit to ___
13. "Scram, varmint!"
14. "Go back" computer command
15. Brain or ear part
16. Stop worrying
18. 35mm camera type
19. Spread, as seed
20. With ice cream
24. Make ___ for oneself
27. Like Pisa's tower
29. Londoner, e.g.
30. Sharp divide
33. Goes over the limit
35. Movie star
36. Thespian's platform
38. Mexican moolah
40. Pencil ends
44. Alan of *Argo*
46. Summer Games org.
47. Equalizer on the links
50. US disaster relief org.
51. Pimples
52. Letter insert: abbr.
53. Even-steven
54. Burn the surface of
55. Ave. crossers
56. Dove or love murmurs

DOWN

1. Model builder's wood
2. Ring-shaped island
3. Actress Winger
4. Extra-wide shoe size
5. Farmer's sci.
6. Fuel for big rigs
7. ___ Helens, Wash.
8. Leaders of hives
9. Not in the know
10. Relatives of egos
11. Yo-yo or Slinky
17. ___ la (singing syllables)
21. Like early Sears business
22. Extra-play periods, for short
23. Lowers, as a light
25. Prefix with day or night
26. Little green men, for short
28. Old Russian monarch
30. Chug's opposite
31. Three after B
32. Biblical cry of praise
34. Nicklaus's org.
37. Renter
39. Move on snow
41. Refrain in "Old MacDonald"
42. Juliet's lover

43. Oodles

45. Frozen treats

47. Contains

48. Top of a royal flush

49. Compaq products

50. Agcy. concerned with false advertising

Solution on Page 260

ACROSS

1. Mo. when spring starts
4. Bat's home
8. Swamps
12. Stanford-Binet nos.
13. "You're making ___ mistake!"
14. "…and pretty maids all in ___"
15. Bust a ___ (laugh hard)
16. Ding's partner
17. Bryant of the NBA
18. Dish under a teacup
20. Touch, taste, or sight, e.g.
21. Stick on
24. Rock of comedy
27. Cry from Homer Simpson
28. Elec. bill unit
31. Reduce to rubble
32. Blue bird
33. Sheltered bay
34. Slangy assent
35. Move one's tail
36. Wide
37. "Am not!" rejoinder
39. Burn badly
43. ___ de corps
47. Court plea, for short
48. Soapmaking substances
50. Make an inquiry
51. Miseries
52. Femur or fibula
53. Letters after L
54. ___ moss
55. Pleasures
56. Opposite of neg.

DOWN

1. Russian fighter jets
2. Pastel blue
3. Q–V connection
4. West Pointers
5. Cancel the launch
6. Actor Diesel
7. Fabergé collectible
8. Use the oven
9. "Straight ___ the rocks?"
10. Lots
11. Popeye's ___' Pea
19. Abel's assassin
20. Librarian's admonition
22. Wise saying
23. Coquettish
24. "___ Me a River"
25. Color tone
26. Tear apart
28. "Kitchy-kitchy-___!"
29. Charleston's st.
30. "I knew a man Bojangles and ___ dance for you…"
32. Jelly container
33. Trim, as a photograph

35. Mouthful of gum

36. Supervisors

38. Itsy-bitsy

39. Cut with scissors

40. ___ slaw

41. "It was ___ mistake"

42. Needing directions

44. Wheelchair access

45. "That ___ excuse!"

46. Ring decisions

48. President after JFK

49. ___-hoo (chocolate drink)

Solution on Page 261

ACROSS

1. Green Bay Packers' org.
4. Luau instrument, informally
7. Elite invitee roster
12. Capote's nickname
13. Half a dozen
14. Raw fish dish
15. Uncomfortable spot
17. Wept
18. "If I Only ___ a Brain"
19. "___ Bailey"
20. Turkey roaster
22. "Do you have two fives for ___?"
24. Place on the payroll
25. Grand Prix, e.g.
30. Corp. execs' degrees
31. Our lang.
32. ___ May of *The Beverly Hillbillies*
33. Watchtower guard
35. Rubber cement, e.g.
36. Went on horseback
37. Barbecue offerings
38. "Cut that out!"
42. Bear's home
43. Luau dances
44. Dance class outfit
48. Actress Dickinson
49. Mercedes competitor
50. Costello or Grant
51. Makes well
52. Snow melter
53. Soapmaking solution

DOWN

1. To the ___ power
2. To and ___ (back and forth)
3. Follower of a German Protestant
4. Exploited
5. Hyundai rival
6. No. after a phone no.
7. Go up
8. Artificial bait
9. "What time ___?"
10. Writer/illustrator Silverstein
11. ___ over (carry through)
16. Most reasonable
19. Snoopy, for one
20. Resistance units
21. Slangy feeling
22. "We ___ amused"
23. ___ down (softened)
26. Feel sorry about
27. Everything considered
28. Driver or putter
29. Holes in needles
34. Van Gogh subjects
38. Former ruler of Iran
39. Adjust the pitch of
40. Gold-medal gymnast Korbut
41. Load for Jack and Jill

42. Pillow filler

44. Abbr. on a dumbbell

45. Big Australian bird

46. Trigger's rider

47. "With all ___ respect…"

Solution on Page 261

ACROSS

1. "The Family Circus" cartoonist Keane
4. Tachometer readings: abbr.
8. In great shape
11. Magnum ___: great work
13. "May ___ you in on a little secret?"
14. Tempe sch.
15. Exercise system from India
16. Dramatic entrance announcement
17. Garment label
18. Authoritative decree
20. Long hikes
22. Innocent ones
25. Circuit protector
27. ___ tree (cornered)
28. Post-accident reassurance
30. Hairless
34. Coupe or sedan
35. More tender
37. Yea's opposite
38. Swiss artist Paul
40. Retort to "Are not!"
41. ___ Another Day (Bond flick)
42. Approximations: abbr.
44. Flies high
46. Wee
49. "For ___ jolly good fellow"
51. Average score
52. "I have ___ good authority"
54. Like some mattresses
58. "___ Wiedersehen" (German goodbye)
59. Ready to be hit, as a golf ball
60. Duck ___ (Marx Brothers film)
61. Prefix meaning "wrong"
62. Smart-alecky talk
63. "That smells disgusting!"

DOWN

1. Lad
2. Stock debut, for short
3. Schlep
4. Sultry Hayworth
5. You may get a rise out of them
6. Club ___ resort
7. Baseball card data
8. Kismet
9. Out of Africa author Dinesen
10. Actions on heartstrings and pant legs
12. Secure
19. Egyptian goddess
21. Yank's foe
22. Greenback
23. "Be ___!" ("Help me out here!")
24. Undecorated
26. Luau instruments, for short
29. Castle's perimeter defense
31. Wing ___ prayer
32. Hibernation location

1	2	3			4	5	6	7		8	9	10
11			12		13					14		
15					16					17		
			18	19				20	21			
22	23	24				25	26					
27				28	29				30	31	32	33
34				35			36		37			
38			39		40				41			
			42	43			44	45				
46	47	48			49	50						
51			52	53			54	55	56	57		
58			59				60					
61			62				63					

33. Salon tints

36. Betsy or Diana

39. Long, thin fish

43. Narrow cuts

45. Bumbling sorts

46. Junk email

47. Hawaii's second-largest island

48. Canine comments

50. They may be split or tight

53. Oolong or Earl Grey

55. Slip signed by a debtor

56. Floor covering

57. Speedometer abbr.

Solution on Page 261

ACROSS

1. Shar-___ (dog)
4. Burger roll
7. Takes to court
11. Rand who wrote *Atlas Shrugged*
12. Civil rights icon Parks
13. "Waiter, there's a fly ___ soup!"
14. HS equivalency test
15. Force from office
16. Ran away from
17. Draw out
19. To the rear, on a ship
21. Fit for a king
22. TV collie
23. 2,000 pounds
24. Morse code click
25. Like a fox
26. Most blue
30. Thus ___ (up to now)
33. Took a match to
34. Old TV knob abbr.
37. Alpaca cousins
39. Was concerned
41. Not in attendance
42. Spin on an axis
43. Big shots, for short
44. Soon
46. Helpful hint
47. ___ Day (vitamin brand)
48. Front-page stuff
49. Toronto's province: abbr.
50. Fishing poles
51. Boob tubes
52. Cheerleader's syllable

DOWN

1. Beeper
2. Hole for a lace
3. Deep blue
4. Boxing match
5. ___ Constitution
6. Actress Portman
7. Searches (through)
8. Except if
9. Lagasse of the Food Network
10. Australia's largest city
12. Agitate
18. Containers
20. HS seniors' exams
24. *Silent Spring* pesticide
27. Actor Alda
28. Aloof
29. This and ___
30. Baskin-Robbins choice
31. Lacking pigment
32. Spoke roughly
35. Rhetorician
36. Light-sensitive eye part
38. Monument Valley features
39. Hoodwinks

40. Third dimension

42. Columns' counterparts

45. Calif. neighbor

Solution on Page 261

ACROSS

1. Craze
4. Hang around for
9. Cookie-selling grp.
12. ___ glance (quickly)
13. Michaels of *SNL*
14. President after Jimmy
15. Smoking or ___? (waiter's query)
16. Country singer Buck
17. "Solve for x" subj.
18. Crystal ball users
20. Small bit
22. Snaky letter
24. Very perceptive
27. Ugly duckling, ultimately
30. Mike and ___ (candy brand)
32. Postal delivery
33. Time Warner spinoff of '09
34. High-___ monitor
35. Phone no.
36. Rich soil
38. Musician Brian
39. Song word repeated after "Que"
40. Break out of jail
42. Winter clock setting in S.F.
44. Santa ___, Calif.
45. Oohed and ___
49. Incoming flight: abbr.
51. Break one's silence
55. "___ the land of the free…"
56. Long.'s opposite
57. Actor McQueen
58. Maiden name signaler
59. Finder's charge
60. Lessens, as pain
61. Hosp. brain readout

DOWN

1. Devotees
2. Stick ___ in the water
3. Copenhagen native
4. At ___ (puzzled)
5. "I'm impressed!"
6. "When Irish Eyes ___ Smiling"
7. Bed-and-breakfast, e.g.
8. Midterms, e.g.
9. Cap and gown wearer
10. Spain's Costa del ___
11. *Hulk* director Lee
19. Stimpy's pal
21. Money machine, for short
23. "Yes ___, Bob!"
24. Fable writer
25. Seating level
26. Fitzgerald known as the First Lady of Song
27. Half-off event
28. Courts
29. Individually, on a menu
31. Kesey who wrote *One Flew Over the Cuckoo's Nest*

37. Fellow

39. Train stop: abbr.

41. So last year

43. "Land ___!"

46. Sharpen, as a razor

47. Extreme shoe width

48. Bit of residue

49. Furry sitcom alien

50. Filmdom's *Norma* ___

52. School fundraising grp.

53. Widish shoe sizes

54. Madison in NYC, e.g.

Solution on Page 262

ACROSS

1. "___ lighter note…"
4. "By the power vested ___…"
8. "Alice's Restaurant" singer Guthrie
12. Newsstand buy, for short
13. Constricting snakes
14. Wanton look
15. Beatles' Pepper rank
17. ___ all-time high
18. ___-or situation
19. Actor Robert De ___
20. Lime drinks
22. *The ___ Express*
24. Maze-running rodent
25. Wise sayings
28. Prefix with thermal or metric
29. Stitched
30. Viet ___
33. Warning devices
34. Endo's opposite
35. "Relax, soldier!"
38. "Disco Duck" singer Rick
39. Catches
40. Was not renewed
44. Brewery products
45. Utopian
48. Apple center
49. Pull back the hammer
50. The Continent: abbr.
51. Some explosives
52. Head shakers' syllables
53. Hitter's stat

DOWN

1. Sounds of meditation
2. "No way, laddie!"
3. Accept
4. "Yeah, right!"
5. Genesis mariner
6. Horse hair
7. Female hormone
8. Grammy winner Morissette
9. Fix a shoelace
10. Acquire knowledge
11. "Ready ___, here…"
16. Enlistees
20. Bush press secretary Fleischer
21. *___ Boot* (1981 war film)
23. Ruby and scarlet
25. Seller's stipulation
26. Vagrant
27. Reverent feeling
30. More impoverished
31. Tree-toppling tool
32. May and June: abbr.
33. Gives some lip
35. Put on ___ (pretend)
36. Eagle's claw
37. Movie critic Roger
38. Wilmington's state: abbr.

41. Fusses

42. Legendary actor Gregory

43. Fifth Avenue landmark

46. Sizable sandwich

47. Prefix for cycle or angle

Solution on Page 262

ACROSS

1. "I don't know yet," on a schedule
4. Gourmet mushroom
9. Baseball hat
12. "This means ___!"
13. Speed skater ___ Anton Ohno
14. Hospital area: abbr.
15. Ideology
16. Water pistol
18. Nephew's sister
20. ___-masochism
21. Support, as a candidate
23. *SportsCenter* channel
27. Swimmer's unit
28. Skin art
30. Make null and void
33. Runs off to marry
34. Like some humor
35. St. Louis clock setting
36. Egg on
37. Selects
41. Jazzy singer ___ James
44. Get through to
45. Start of a Christmas letter
49. Rock music's ___ Fighters
50. Heart chart, for short
51. Unadorned
52. Ltr. holder
53. Happened upon
54. Peddles
55. ___ v. Wade (1973 Supreme Court decision)

DOWN

1. Packing string
2. Place to wash up
3. Prepared for battle
4. Ferrari rival
5. N–R connection
6. Awaken
7. Film director Kazan
8. ___ of the Flies
9. Smoke, for short
10. Prefix with puncture
11. Bit of wordplay
17. Direct, as a confrontation
19. Container for draining and straining
22. On ___ (without a buyer)
24. Engine additive brand
25. "The Raven" poet
26. Phone book listings: abbr.
28. ___ support (help for computer users)
29. Distant finishers
30. Little bite
31. Make a gaffe
32. Viscous substance
37. Artificial waterway
38. More secure

1	2	3		4	5	6	7	8		9	10	11
12				13						14		
15				16					17			
18			19				20					
21					22				23	24	25	26
			27					28	29			
30	31	32					33					
34							35					
36						37				38	39	40
			41	42	43			44				
45	46	47					48			49		
50				51						52		
53				54						55		

39. ___ Lodge (motel chain)

40. Rudely push

42. Baking soda amts.

43. Shakespeare's *The Winter's* ___

45. Not Rep. or Ind.

46. ___ out (barely manage)

47. Actor's rep.

48. "Shop ___ you drop"

Solution on Page 262

ACROSS

1. Col. Sanders's chain
4. Cookbook meas.
7. N. ___ (Fargo's state, for short)
10. Breakfast restaurant chain
12. Laments
14. Alternative to .com or .net
15. Broadway auntie
16. ___-date (current)
17. ___-tickler (funny joke)
18. Homes on wheels, in brief
20. Washington's successor
22. Find not guilty
25. CA airport
26. "...life is ___ a dream"
27. ___ XING (street sign)
29. Truck stop stoppers
33. Term paper abbr.
35. "There's a mouse!"
37. Tyne of *Cagney & Lacey*
38. Wigwam relative
40. Opposite of masc.
42. Get a blue ribbon
43. Attorneys' degs.
45. "Ditto!"
47. Wood finish
49. "Bad" cholesterol letters
50. Dylan or Dole
51. Chickens and turkeys
53. Radio letters
57. Conditions
58. It has its ups and downs
59. Parcel (out)
60. Hit with a stun gun
61. ___ favor: please (Sp.)
62. *How the West Was* ___ (1962)

DOWN

1. "Bette Davis Eyes" singer Carnes
2. Loan org.
3. Dot-___ (Internet company)
4. College board member
5. Have dinner
6. Flower feature
7. College digs
8. Fleischer and Onassis
9. Cold War spy org.
11. Lima's country
13. Fountain drinks
19. Big shot, briefly
21. Took a hatchet to
22. "This won't hurt ___!"
23. Six-sided solid
24. Ear cleaner
28. Dictionary entry: abbr.
30. Bryn ___ College
31. Tennis champ Nastase
32. "Auld Lang ___"
34. ___ vu

36. Garrison of *A Prairie Home Companion*
39. Uplift spiritually
41. Very angry
44. Nosy one
46. Contented
47. Parlor seat
48. Recipe amt.

50. "That's show ___!"
52. Casper's st.
54. Level out the lawn
55. ___-Jo (1988 Olympics star)
56. Sign on a bathroom door

Solution on Page 262

ACROSS

1. Beach shades
5. Wooden pin
8. Fountain pen filler
11. "Stupid ___ stupid does"
12. Build up a nest egg
13. Billiards stick
14. McGregor of *Down with Love*
15. Goatee's locale
16. Approved
17. Motion detector, e.g.
19. Construction site machines
21. Bother
23. Dog doc
26. Greek T
27. Dairy animals
31. "___ put our heads together…"
33. *The Ghost and ___ Muir*
35. Bob of *Road* films
36. Jim Croce's "___ a Name"
37. Salon stiffener
39. Send via phone line
40. Facet
43. Embodiment
46. Cleans the blackboard
51. *Jaws* sighting
52. Fend (off)
54. Songbird
55. Baton Rouge sch.
56. *The Sopranos* Emmy winner Falco
57. Do a slow burn
58. As ___ (so far)
59. Father figure
60. "There oughta be ___!"

DOWN

1. Trash bag closers
2. "…___ forgive our debtors…"
3. Indian flatbread
4. Tax form IDs
5. Oom___
6. Oust
7. Literary category
8. Computer image
9. Microwave
10. Popular sneakers
12. Sound of fright
18. ___ out (decline)
20. Curved gateway
22. Swell
23. Seven, on a sundial
24. Three after D
25. Duo
28. Sock-in-the-gut grunt
29. New Deal org.
30. Topic for Dr. Ruth
32. Coup d'___
34. Withdraw (from)
38. Env. contents
41. Cut wood

42. *The Devil Wears* ___

43. ___ in the ointment

44. Tool with jaws

45. "Sometimes you feel like ___..."

47. ___ Romeo (Italian auto)

48. *Herzog* author Bellow

49. Humor columnist Bombeck

50. Twist, as facts

53. Get ___ of (discard)

Solution on Page 263

ACROSS

1. ___ tai (drink)
4. Jackson 5 hairdo
8. The ___ (awful)
12. Ending with east or west
13. Neighbor of Thailand
14. Saturn feature
15. Byways: abbr.
16. Felt-tip alternative
18. Crystal-lined rock
20. Leopold's partner in crime
21. Compel obedience to
23. Happen again
27. Thespian
28. A musing sound
29. Poland's capital
31. Humiliate
34. Once ___ blue moon
35. Dairy Queen purchases
36. Shopping aids
39. Stretchy, as a waistband
42. Frau's spouse
44. Country estate
45. Toupee
49. One: Fr.
50. "No thanks, ___ already"
51. Music's McCartney
52. Casual Friday castoff
53. Tobacco plug
54. Elegant shade trees
55. Despondent

DOWN

1. Join forces
2. Elizabeth of cosmetics
3. To the degree that
4. Edmonton's province
5. Air safety org.
6. Paintbrush alternative
7. Capital of Norway
8. Investigate
9. The Third
10. Old cable inits.
11. Lt.'s subordinate
17. ___ diem (daily allowance)
19. Medics
22. Mooer
24. "___ roasting on an open fire"
25. *Pulp Fiction* actress Thurman
26. LBJ's successor
29. Wheaton of *Star Trek: The Next Generation*
30. *Star Wars: Episode I—The Phantom Menace* boy
31. US currency
32. Nail and tooth coverings
33. Flat-topped mountain
35. Breakfast food

37. Pitched

38. Calendar abbr.

40. Ancient Aegean land

41. Guiding principle

43. Ready to be harvested

45. Drunk's sound

46. Sigh of delight

47. Give ___ whirl (try)

48. Magna ___ laude

Solution on Page 263

ACROSS

1. Family docs
4. Walker's aid
8. Prepare, as a salad
12. Put to good ___
13. Elvis's middle name
14. "It's a Sin to Tell ___"
15. Taoism founder Lao ___
16. Frees (of)
17. Copper coin
18. Alternative to a paper clip
20. Creaks and squeaks
22. "___ in apple"
23. Garfunkel or Carney
24. Like ___ out of hell
27. Prefix meaning "before"
28. Suffix with lime or lemon
31. Atlas contents
32. Had dinner
33. Mimicked
34. Driveway covering
35. Capt.'s inferiors
36. Foldable beds
37. *Good Will Hunting* school
38. Occupied a chair
40. Tex-Mex snack
43. Trouser leg measurement
47. Color tones
48. Alphabetize
50. ___ Khan (Islamic title)
51. Fateful day in March
52. Arbor Day honoree
53. Take ___ (rest)
54. Building lot
55. Hourglass fill
56. "Try ___ might…"

DOWN

1. Courage, informally
2. Whispered "Hey!"
3. "I ___ bad moon rising"
4. Rhea's role on *Cheers*
5. Sign before Taurus
6. Land of ___
7. Catch in a trap
8. Unspoken
9. Shouts for the matador
10. ___ qua non
11. Goes down, as the sun
19. Butter squares
21. Mine yield
24. Tbsp. or tsp.
25. Word repeated before "black sheep"
26. Fourth mo.
27. Scoreboard nos.
28. Part of a GI's address
29. Investigator: abbr.
30. Asner and Begley
32. Certifies under oath

33. Does stage work

35. "___ ol' me?"

37. En ___ (as a group)

38. Ambulance sound

39. ___ up (paid)

40. "Get a load of ___!"

41. Car with a four-ring logo

42. Track-and-field contest

44. ___ *Peach* (Allman Brothers album)

45. Puts on years

46. ___-pedi

49. "…blessing ___ curse?"

Solution on Page 263

ACROSS

1. The Dalai ___
5. Drill insert
8. Tease playfully
11. Open ___ of worms
12. "___ du lieber!"
13. Not ___ many words
14. Disney's ___ & *Stitch*
15. Bill ___, the Science Guy
16. Without an escort
17. Deviates from the script
19. The "S" in CBS
21. Opposite of "yeah"
22. College website suffix
23. Acorn producer
27. Letter flourish
31. When repeated, a Gabor
32. Christmas toymaker
34. 201, to Caesar
35. Went undercover
38. Boo-boo
41. Young dog
43. *Morning Edition* airer
44. One's life story
47. Inviting smells
51. NYSE rival
52. Texter's "Unbelievable!"
54. Way through the woods
55. Breezy
56. Zero, in soccer
57. "Am ___ late?"
58. VH1 alternative
59. Sr.'s test
60. Pitch a tent

DOWN

1. In ___ land (dreaming)
2. The "A" in DNA
3. Retail complex
4. Consecrate with oil
5. Wailer of Irish folklore
6. Slick
7. "One of ___ days…"
8. Macrame feature
9. Ireland, the Emerald ___
10. Dire prophecy
13. Debate topic
18. Mixologist's workplace
20. Fabric amts.
23. Parts of lbs.
24. Snake along the Nile
25. China's Chiang ___-shek
26. Sturdy tree
28. Major TV brand
29. "That's gross!"
30. "For shame!"
33. Achieve through trickery
36. Powerful adhesive
37. Charge that makes MADD mad
39. Easter season: abbr.

40. ___ of Capricorn

42. Fork tine

44. Sir's partner

45. Give off, as rays

46. TV's Griffin

48. Spy ___ Hari

49. Proton's place

50. Boutique

53. Fallen space station

Solution on Page 263

ACROSS

1. Imposter
5. Escape, as from jail
8. Alphabetical start
12. Hydrant hookup
13. Lacto-___ vegetarian
14. Rice-A-___
15. Said aloud
16. Where to get a taxi
18. Amer. currency unit
19. Soundness of mind
20. Stovetop whistler
22. Bread for a Reuben
25. Intense wrath
26. More spine-tingling
28. Where hair roots grow
31. Glass squares
32. Hang around
34. Pol with a six-yr. term
35. Like a geriatrician's patient
36. Essential
41. "It's about time!"
42. August zodiac sign
43. Scotch mixer
46. ___-deucey (card game)
47. Long-eared leaper
48. Sling's contents
49. Sport with mallets
50. Tip-top
51. Near-failing grade
52. Avoid flunking

DOWN

1. Yell
2. Palomino or Clydesdale
3. Carne ___ (Mexican restaurant dish)
4. Blanc or Brooks
5. Find
6. ___-garde
7. Delicately balanced artwork
8. Pretentiously styled
9. Constricting snake
10. Atlanta-based news channel
11. Carried out
17. Least gradual
19. Slithering hissers
21. Bagpiper's wear
22. ___ Tin Tin (heroic dog of 1950s TV)
23. "___-haw!" (rodeo cry)
24. Hosp. triage areas
27. Also-___ (losers)
28. ___-mo camera
29. Newspaper div.
30. Good Samaritan's offering
33. Insert fresh cartridges
34. Big Bird's street

PUZZLE 25

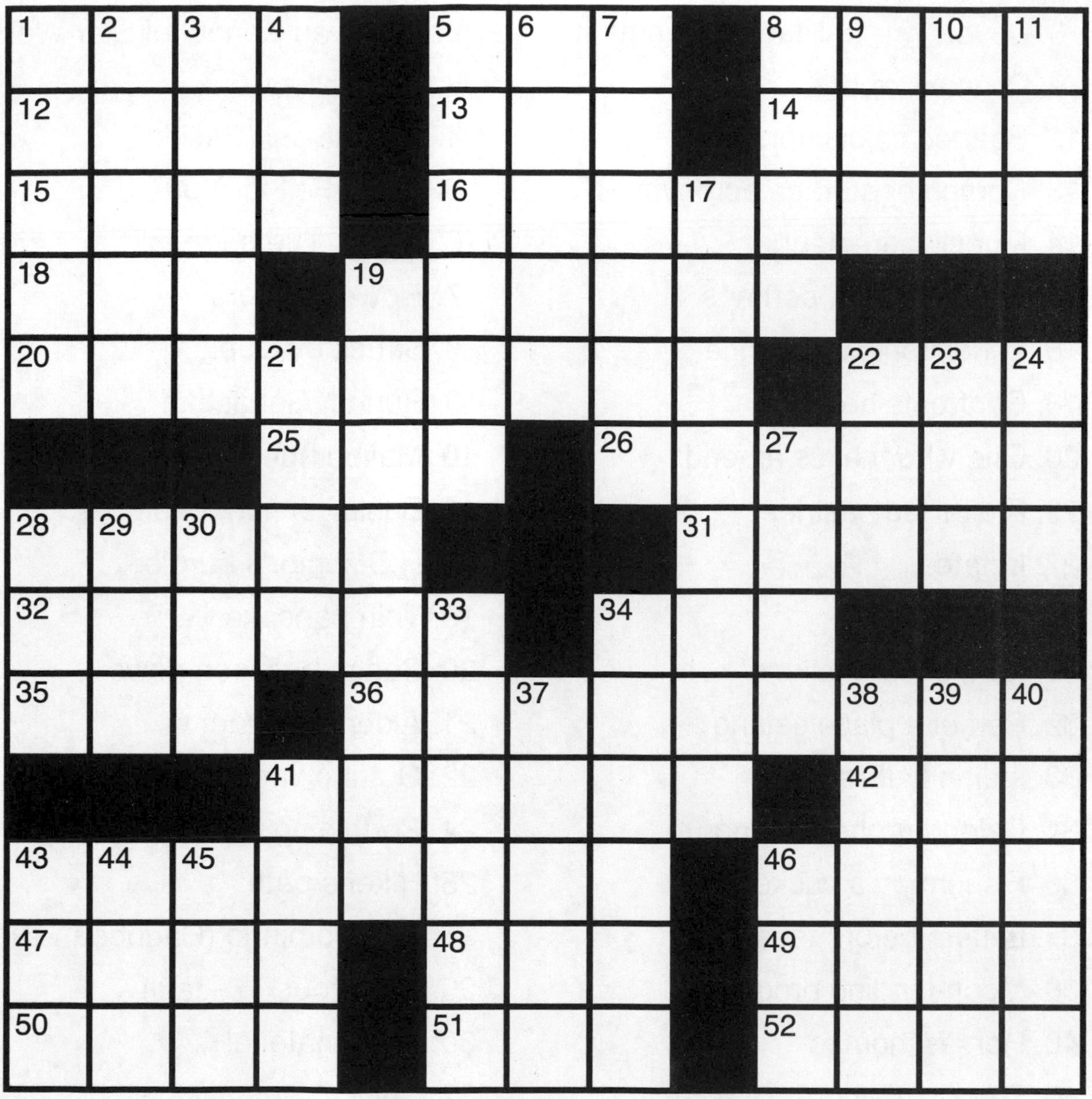

37. Group of key officers
38. Foil maker
39. Film vault collection
40. Toys on strings
41. Have ___ in one's bonnet
43. Half a Latin dance
44. Philosopher ___ Tzu
45. Cremains holder
46. PC program, briefly

Solution on Page 264

ACROSS

1. Goes it alone
6. Covert ___ (military assignments)
9. Pennies: abbr.
12. Beaded calculators
13. Computer storage acronym
14. Muesli ingredient
15. Add a lane to, perhaps
16. Scholarship allowance
18. Confronts boldly
20. One who makes amends
23. Fruit-filled pastries
27. Irritates
28. And so forth
31. Sun. church talk
32. Part of a place setting
33. Indian flatbread
34. Calendar phenomenon
36. Fisherman's bucketful
37. Letters before tees
38. Moon-landing program
40. Horses' homes
43. *The ___ Falcon*
46. Queen ___ lace
50. Toothpaste-endorsing org.
51. Wire measure
52. "Would I ___ you?"
53. Stubborn animal
54. Arch city: abbr.
55. Bother persistently

DOWN

1. Observed
2. ___-Wan Kenobi of Star Wars
3. Wee fellow
4. Atlantic and Pacific
5. "___ I Fell for You"
6. "…___ I've been told"
7. Flower holders
8. Struck by Cupid
9. Runner Sebastian
10. Malibu hue
11. Basic version: abbr.
17. H.S. junior's hurdle
19. Thin pancake
20. Space between pews
21. Alder and elder
22. Gumbo vegetables
24. Pertaining to the kidneys
25. Hiker's path
26. ___ Domingo (Caribbean capital)
29. Generous ___ fault
30. Reef material
32. "All ___ go!"
35. Nuisance
36. Neighbor of Croatia
39. Positive thinker Norman Vincent ___
41. ___ were (seemingly)
42. Ringer
43. Lamb's bleat

44. Billboard messages

45. ___ Vegas, Nevada

47. Income after deductions

48. Expected landing hr.

49. Barfly

Solution on Page 264

ACROSS

1. ___ for tat
4. ___-ray Disc
7. Police radio alert, briefly
10. Enter the water headfirst
11. Cut (off), as with a sweeping motion
12. Check the age of
14. Partner of Crackle and Pop
15. "Every dog has ___ day"
16. Tax pros: abbr.
17. Not strict
19. Minimum amount
20. Netflix mailing
21. Hit on the head
22. Kind of PC monitor
25. Helper
30. Opera song
32. ___ out (overeat)
33. ___-in (certain victor)
34. Sidewalk game
37. "Were ___ do it over…"
38. Extinguish, with "out"
39. That man
41. Mr. Fudd
44. Leaves
48. Raise, as kids
49. Cohort of Curly and Larry
50. Knocker's place
51. Lawyers: abbr.
52. ER hookups
53. Play's opening
54. Pronoun for a ship
55. Dee's predecessor
56. Daisy ___ of *Li'l Abner*

DOWN

1. Fork part
2. "Terrible" czar
3. Barely warm
4. Lane changer's danger
5. Mississippi's Trent
6. ___ and downs
7. Agrees to
8. Biggest of the Three Bears
9. Playtex products
10. High-speed Internet inits.
13. Summer clock setting: abbr.
18. ___ Perón, former Argentine first lady
19. ___ Angeles Dodgers
21. Head honcho
22. "Well, ___-di-dah!"
23. ___-Magnon (early human)
24. Potato chip accompaniment
26. Plop down
27. Sushi bar tuna
28. *Ripley's Believe It or ___!*
29. ___ many irons in the fire
31. Slander

64

35. Junkyard dog

36. Cool or groovy

40. Lady's title

41. Period in history

42. David Bowie's "___ Dance"

43. SAT section

44. Winged peace symbol

45. Almond ___ (candy brand)

46. Pledge drive bag

47. ___ Lankan

49. Tape rec. jack

Solution on Page 264

ACROSS

1. "I'd be glad to"
4. Numbered hwys.
8. Gillette razor
12. Certain vote
13. Lighten up
14. Dove or Dial
15. "I pity the fool" star
16. Wheel rotator
17. Heavenly music maker
18. Hand-holding, spirit-raising get-together
20. Behind the ___
22. "___ be my pleasure!"
23. Apt. coolers
24. Bank no.
27. Cries of pain
28. Newsman Donaldson
31. Cattle calls
32. Jobs for grad students
33. Scarlett's plantation
34. S&L offerings
35. ___ choy (Chinese green)
36. Raggedy Ann's friend
37. On Soc. Sec.
38. Flow away, as a tide
40. Conditional release
43. Partner of cease
47. Word of woe
48. Garden plots
50. Scooby-___ (cartoon dog)
51. "You've got ___ nerve!"
52. Landed
53. "Don't mind if ___"
54. Big name in elevators
55. Travels
56. Not dis

DOWN

1. Thanksgiving side dish
2. *Jane* ___
3. ___ precedent
4. Respond to a stimulus
5. Imposed a levy on
6. Class for US immigrants
7. Teeter-totters
8. Fireplace residue
9. Means ___ end
10. Lightly cooked
11. Downloadable programs
19. Things to pick
21. Syringe amts.
24. Rambler mfr.
25. Atlantic food fish
26. Firms: abbr.
27. Source of acorns
28. ___ Antonio, Tex.
29. Suffix with dull or drunk
30. Spring month
32. Carryall

33. Day planner features

35. Actress Barbara ___ Geddes

37. Kentucky Derby flowers

38. Fisher or Foy

39. Outdoes in competition

40. El ___, Tex.

41. Oodles and oodles

42. *Bohemian Rhapsody* star Malek

44. "Look what ___!"

45. Word after baking or club

46. Choo-choo's sound

49. "Strange Magic" grp.

Solution on Page 264

ACROSS

1. Companion for Tarzan
4. Labor Day mo.
8. Whole bunch
12. Louse-to-be
13. Early late-night host
14. Bathroom flooring
15. ___ Offensive (Vietnam War event)
16. "Look ___ when I'm talking to you!"
17. Very small batteries
18. Tea leaves reader
20. Retired sonic boom producer
22. "A ___ formality!"
25. "You can ___ horse to…"
29. Taxis
32. Like falling off a log
34. Beirut's land: abbr.
35. Have another birthday
36. Bushy hairdos
37. ___ kwon do (martial art)
38. Greyhound stop: abbr.
39. Pie pans
40. ___ serif (font choice)
41. Item of value
43. Encl. with a manuscript
45. Amniotic ___
47. Alternatives to PCs
50. "I ___ my wit's end"
53. Ready, willing, and ___
56. Neighbor of Ger.
58. Boy or man
59. Screwdriver, e.g.
60. *In Dreams* actor Stephen
61. Soaks (up)
62. Santa soiler
63. Dada artist Jean

DOWN

1. Tiny hill builder
2. Pecan and pumpkin
3. Suffix with luncheon
4. Tire in the trunk
5. Have breakfast
6. Cooking spray brand
7. Uno + dos
8. Governor's domain
9. Spying org.
10. Tuscaloosa's state: abbr.
11. ___ Moines, IA
19. Followers of els
21. Stone and Stallone
23. Mortgage adjustment, for short
24. Makes, as a salary
26. ___Vista (Internet search engine)
27. Martin of the Rat Pack
28. Vigoda and Lincoln
29. Spanish house
30. 007 and others: abbr.
31. Uncle ___ (rice brand)
33. Sammy with three 60-homer seasons
36. "___ boy!" ("Way to go!")

40. ___ of Tranquility (where the Eagle landed)
42. ___ Park, Colo.
44. Refine, as metal
46. Lions and tigers
48. Singer Irene
49. Litigious sort

50. Mornings, for short
51. Longtime Chinese chairman
52. Continental peak
54. Halloween word
55. Brit's bathroom
57. Source of maple syrup

Solution on Page 265

ACROSS

1. Mix with a swizzle stick
5. Attila's horde
9. Declare verboten
12. Pepsi competitor
13. A Great Lake
14. *Ally McBeal* actress Lucy
15. Take down ___ (demote)
16. Merlot, for one
17. Blast producer
18. Martini & ___ vermouth
20. Sail holders
22. Stock exchange worker
26. Gift container
29. ___ avail (hopeless)
30. "I say, old ___"
34. Billiard sticks
36. Football six-pointers, for short
37. Japanese wrestling
38. "Where ___ go wrong?"
39. City near Provo, Utah
41. To the ___ (fully)
42. Most uncommon
44. Stun gun
47. Chip dip
52. "May ___ of service?"
53. Shortened wd.
57. Pile
58. Partner of games
59. Keeps out
60. Sandwich spread
61. 1-800-FLOWERS rival
62. Flu season protection
63. Timeline periods

DOWN

1. Reminder of an injury
2. "___ the mornin' to you!"
3. Turner and Eisenhower
4. Rules, for short
5. Cut down
6. Controversial mentalist Geller
7. *Henry & June* diarist
8. "If they could ___ now…"
9. Layered sandwiches, for short
10. "___ No Mountain High Enough" (1970 #1 hit)
11. Loony
19. *The Addams Family* cousin
21. Parabolic paths
23. Spinning part
24. Tennis star Agassi
25. Units of medicine
26. A followers
27. Yes, in Paris
28. Canceled, with "out"
31. Engine sound
32. Simon and Garfunkel's "I ___ Rock"
33. Plague
35. Father

40. Shasta and Olympus, for short

43. Many Mideasterners

44. Petty quarrel

45. Share a border with

46. Mail off

48. "Whatever shall I do?"

49. Kind of jet

50. "I ___ Little Prayer" (Dionne Warwick hit)

51. Mil. mail centers

54. Scrooge's "Phooey!"

55. Sibling for sis

56. Queue before U

Solution on Page 265

ACROSS

1. Prone (to)
4. Cries of triumph
8. Sacha Baron Cohen character
12. "…or ___ thought"
13. TV newsman Brit
14. Sewing line
15. Part of a circle
16. Eyelid annoyance
17. Shade of color
18. Cuban money
20. Pet adoption org.
22. ___ good deed daily
25. Go off like a volcano
29. Ore-Ida product
34. *Cannery* ___
35. "May ___ now?"
36. Divas' solos
37. ___ long way (last)
38. Snoop
39. The 8 in V8
41. Rope fiber
43. PC grouping
44. Church offshoot
47. Run ___ (accumulate debt at a bar)
51. Designer Saint Laurent
54. Young of Crosby, Stills, Nash & Young
57. You ___ (one of us)
58. Leeds's river
59. Acid's opposite
60. Driver's license stat.
61. Fannie ___ (securities)
62. Lit ___ (English major's class)
63. "How ___ love thee?"

DOWN

1. "This can't wait!"
2. Go (over) carefully
3. Uncontrollable movements
4. Cries at fireworks
5. Humble home
6. Vanderbilt and Grant
7. Trickle (through)
8. ___ *Is Born*
9. Gift that may be presented with an "Aloha!"
10. Fleming who created James Bond
11. Clock standard: abbr.
19. "___ to Billy Joe"
21. Big name in small planes
23. Prophet at Delphi
24. Give it ___ (attempt)
26. Encourage
27. Needy
28. "___ the night before Christmas…"
29. Helpful hints
30. Prefix with culture
31. Aerosmith album ___ *in the Attic*
32. Squeak silencer
33. Kite stabilizer
40. What identical twins have in common

42. Beasts of burden

45. Business TV channel

46. Something shed

48. Rocker Rundgren

49. Suffix with buck

50. Netanyahu, familiarly

51. Candied veggie

52. Going by way of

53. Before, in poems

55. "It ___" (formal answer to "Who's there?")

56. ___ go (release)

Solution on Page 265

ACROSS

1. ___ Holiness the Pope
4. Slinky's shape
8. Tot's recitation
12. Mean Amin
13. Hyundai or Honda
14. "___ ever so humble…"
15. Pre-K enrollee
16. Baby bed
17. "There wasn't ___ eye in the house!"
18. Tallow source
20. Weep aloud
22. Candle cord
25. Monte ___, Monaco
29. Macpherson of *Sirens*
32. Café au ___
34. ___ Lingus (carrier to Dublin)
35. No middle ground, successwise
38. The 2% in 2% milk
39. Gorillas and chimps
40. Aardvark snacks
41. Trapshooting
43. Overly inquisitive
45. English majors' degs.
47. Baseball hats
50. Workout centers
53. King novel about a rabid dog
56. The ___ Four (The Beatles)
58. Goodyear product
59. Way off
60. Govt. Rx watchdog
61. "What's going ___ there?"
62. West German capital
63. Chairman pro ___

DOWN

1. Box office smash
2. They're exchanged at the altar
3. In ___ (in its original position)
4. Desert plants
5. Yours and mine
6. "Lord, is ___?" (Last Supper question)
7. Lofty tennis shots
8. Addis ___, Ethiopia
9. Part of B&B
10. Round: abbr.
11. Pig's abode
19. Providers of sheep's milk
21. Quadri- times two
23. Horse-hoof sound
24. Grammy winner Carpenter
26. Drought ender
27. Pre-Easter season
28. They're mined and refined
29. Letters before gees
30. Plumbing problem
31. Running behind schedule
33. "Assuming that's true…"

PUZZLE 32

36. "Toodle-oo!"
37. Central American Indian
42. *Barnaby Jones* star Buddy
44. Treat with contempt
46. Strike defier
48. "All gone!" sound
49. "No Ordinary Love" singer
50. Pontiac in a '60s hit song
51. Yang partner
52. Hosp. diagnostic
54. Martian's craft, say
55. Winter mo.
57. "Kapow!"

Solution on Page 265

ACROSS

1. Tick-borne disease
5. Peach center
8. "Be with you in a coupla ___"
12. Writing tablets
13. Gardner once married to Sinatra
14. Hand lotion ingredient
15. Part of PBS: abbr.
16. ___-Mex cuisine
17. Heredity carrier
18. Garden of Eden woman
20. Home of Iowa State University
21. Film director Frank
24. Places to be pampered
27. Bullfighting cheer
28. Backs of necks
30. On the ___ (exactly)
33. *Hamilton* creator ___-Manuel Miranda
34. Sits in neutral
35. *Scent* ___ *Woman*
36. Takes too much, for short
37. Parisian river
38. Excavate
39. Atkins of country music
40. Glasgow residents
42. Concerning, in a memo
45. Org. with merit badges
46. Inspires reverence in
47. '50s pres.
49. Uses a sofa
53. Help for the stumped
54. Not home
55. Part of a.k.a.
56. Some NCOs
57. Canon camera named for a goddess
58. Strike with open hand

DOWN

1. Turntable turners, briefly
2. "That's great news!"
3. ER VIPs
4. Fragrant compound
5. Hors d'oeuvres spread
6. "___ been thinking…"
7. April 15 payment
8. Long, drawn-out stories
9. Kind of sch.
10. Volcano shape
11. Matches, as a bet
19. Disappear
21. Denver's st.
22. "Put ___ on it!"
23. Pigs' digs
24. ___-pea soup
25. Ball-___ hammer
26. Evaluate
29. "Zip-___-Doo-Dah"
30. Extinct bird

31. "Wanna make something ___?"

32. Luggage IDs

39. Expenses

41. Spanish houses

42. Satisfied sounds

43. Deep drink

44. Circus structure

45. "All ___ are off!"

47. Bambi's mother, e.g.

48. Hall & Oates, e.g.

50. Down with the flu, say

51. Airport screening org.

52. Soak (up)

Solution on Page 266

ACROSS

1. City map
5. CBS drama
8. "The Bible Tells ___"
12. Make mad
13. "That feels good!"
14. Sign on a store door
15. Sign for the superstitious
16. "Well, I'll ___ monkey's uncle!"
17. Catchall abbr.
18. Kings, queens, and jacks
21. About-face from NNW
22. Waterproof cover
23. *Star Trek: TNG* counselor
25. Free TV ad, for short
28. Educators' org.
29. Fund, as one's alma mater
31. Bothers incessantly
33. Take offense at
34. ___ Island (immigrants' site)
35. Vim and vigor
36. Air-leak sound
37. Diplomatic quality
38. At rest
40. Admission in a confessional
41. Pleasant
46. Golden Rule's second word
48. Set down
49. Travel aimlessly
50. Luke Skywalker's sister
51. Suffix with meteor
52. Zero, on a court
53. The Beatles' "Back in the ___"
54. Wanna-___ (pretenders)
55. Trade punches in training

DOWN

1. Univ. teacher
2. Capital of Peru
3. Smart ___ (wise guy)
4. Church belief
5. Club with a floor show
6. Mount Everest guide
7. "If ___ My Way"
8. Apple pie partner?
9. Sitcom segments
10. Rap or jam periods
11. ___ over lightly
19. Rummy variety
20. Church topper
24. GP's assistants
25. ___ Wee Reese
26. Soup crackers
27. Legendary sunken island
30. Scale amts.
32. [not my error]
33. Overnight flights
35. *Jolly Roger* flier
39. Some noblemen
40. *Star Trek: TOS* helmsman

1	2	3	4		5	6	7		8	9	10	11
12					13				14			
15					16				17			
18				19				20		21		
			22					23	24			
25	26	27		28				29				30
31			32				33					
34						35			36			
	37					38		39				
40				41	42					43	44	45
46			47		48				49			
50					51				52			
53					54				55			

42. Superficially fluent

43. Betty of comics

44. ___ lamp (1960s novelty)

45. Like a 911 call: abbr.

47. Crew blade

Solution on Page 266

ACROSS

1. *The ___ of Pooh*
4. Sound boosters
8. Take out of the freezer
12. Canine cry
13. Ernie's Muppet pal
14. Both: prefix
15. ___-dandy
16. "Pants on fire" fellow
17. "Parlez-___ français?"
18. Boxer Oscar ___ Hoya
20. Christmas season
22. Israeli weapon
24. Intense fear
28. Mountain climber's return
32. Snoozer's sound
33. Animal with antlers
34. Bridge declaration
36. UK television network
37. Track events
40. Competition
43. Get really steamed
45. Cat call
46. ___ tea
48. Texas ___ M
51. Road division
54. Underground part of a plant
56. Kennel sound
58. Great Salt ___
59. Writer's inspiration
60. Arafat's grp.
61. ET transporters
62. Give ___ for one's money
63. Bank acct. entry

DOWN

1. ___ Mahal
2. Extremely dry
3. *All ___* (Steve Martin comedy)
4. On fire
5. "Don't blame ___ voted for…"
6. Appeal to God
7. Walk proudly
8. Alehouse
9. Med. group
10. ___ Dhabi
11. Minn. neighbor
19. Jean-___ Picard
21. *Au Revoir ___ Enfants*
23. Bach's Mass ___ Minor
25. After-bath cover
26. Globes
27. Four-sided fig.
28. Reps.' foes
29. "Waiting for the Robert ___"
30. ___-Ball (amusement park game)
31. ___-*Tac-Dough*
35. Joe DiMaggio's brother
38. Three-wheelers
39. "Hold on just a ___!"

80

41. Spruce up

42. Howard Hughes's airline

44. Skin layer

47. Gloomy

49. Det. Sipowicz's employer

50. Hill's opposite

51. Annual vaccine target

52. Big lug

53. Early MGM rival

55. Columbus campus initials

57. Old man

Solution on Page 266

ACROSS

1. Next of ___
4. Provides with personnel
8. Dictator Idi
12. New pedometer reading
13. King toppers
14. ___ Nostra
15. ___ and outs (intricacies)
16. Cry of relief
17. Big jump
18. Shut tight
20. Evicts
21. *Children of a ___ God*
23. Help a hoodlum
26. Hunting dog
31. Roaming folks
34. Julia's *Seinfeld* role
35. Main order in a restaurant
36. Was aware of
37. Infuse with bubbles
41. Elephant of children's lit
45. The 49th state
48. Rent-___ (security guard)
49. Take ___ (go swimming)
50. Fuse measure
52. Subtle glow
53. "___ a nice day!"
54. "Give ___ kiss!"
55. R.B.I. or H.R.
56. Greek god of war
57. Also

DOWN

1. Colorful pond fish
2. Charged atoms
3. Carrot on a snowman, perhaps
4. Syrup source
5. ___ and pains
6. Necessities
7. Opposite NNE
8. Rights org.
9. *The Simpsons* tavern
10. "Time ___ a premium"
11. Siestas
19. Wedding site
20. Hershiser on the mound
22. Point opposite WNW
23. Most common draw in Scrabble
24. "___ voyage party"
25. CPR pro
27. Seizes
28. Kind of foil
29. Compass point opposite WSW
30. FF's opposite, on a VCR
32. ___ John letter
33. Match, as a bet
38. *M*A*S*H* clerk
39. ___ and kicking

40. Cassettes

41. Sheepish sounds

42. ___ above (better than)

43. Afghanistan's Tora ___ region

44. Get ___ on the back

46. ___ *Sutra*

47. Prayer closer

49. "Mystery solved!"

51. Place for notes

Solution on Page 266

ACROSS

1. Finish, with "up"
4. Seeks answers
8. Congo's cont.
11. Collections of anecdotes
13. Devoted group
14. ___ de Janeiro, Brazil
15. Not good, but not bad
16. "Don't Tread ___" (old flag warning)
17. Height: abbr.
18. Cops enforce them
20. Pays to play poker
22. ___-toothed tiger
25. Easter roasts
27. From ___ Z (completely): 2 wds.
28. Electric or water co.
30. Actress Jessica
34. ___ rummy
35. Armored vehicles
37. Order to a firing squad
38. Chair
40. Authentic
41. Make dove sounds
42. Horse food
44. Bottomless pit
46. Instances
49. Docile
51. Drink that may accompany fish and chips
52. Stocking tear
54. Sound of a leak
58. Sought political office
59. Short letter
60. Neuter, as a pet
61. Sonny's sibling
62. Zipped along
63. Hither and ___

DOWN

1. Bell and Kettle, e.g.
2. Musical Yoko
3. Mas' partners
4. "Don't have ___, man!"
5. Florida nickname
6. Airline to Holland
7. Fulton's power
8. Smell ___ (be wary)
9. Use an emery board on
10. Becomes compost
12. Boot bottom
19. In ___ (going nowhere)
21. Top-secret org.
22. Gives in to gravity
23. End in ___ (finish evenly)
24. ___ fide (authentic)
26. ___-Seltzer (antacid brand)
29. Fruity pastry
31. Like some lingerie
32. Life stories, for short
33. Famous ___ (cookie brand)

36. Close loudly
39. Swimming pool tester
43. Orgs.
45. Mrs. Truman
46. Detroit products
47. Jai ___ (fast-moving sport)
48. DC 100: abbr.

50. Ripened
53. Trio before Q
55. Engage in espionage
56. ___ Paulo (Brazil's most populous city)
57. Opposite of ant.

Solution on Page 267

ACROSS

1. "___ were you…"
4. "___ I cared!"
8. Urban renewal target
12. Sewing basket item
13. Janet in the Clinton White House
14. Musical sound
15. Mexican seaport known for its cliff divers
17. Rolling in dough
18. River in a Strauss waltz
19. Pairs
21. Table salt
23. Acquired relative
26. School grps.
29. Kind of pregame party
31. Leather-piercing tool
32. Short-tempered
33. Fall mo.
34. Turbulent currents
36. ___ Le Pew
37. Traffic tie-up
38. Chest rattle
40. Use the phone
42. Ten dimes
46. Fashionable
48. Musical opening
50. Uncle's wife
51. "See what I ___?"
52. Disney frame
53. Warner ___
54. Dracula portrayer Lugosi
55. Mary ___ cosmetics

DOWN

1. Apple tablet computer
2. Paycheck deduction
3. "I knew ___ instant…"
4. Caribbean resort island
5. Picked out
6. Small-business magazine
7. ___ the bill: pay
8. Brawny
9. *Daily Planet* reporter
10. Dad's bro
11. "I'm not impressed"
16. Groan-inducing jokes
20. Sly
22. Modern surgical tool
24. At the pinnacle of
25. "___ Got Tonight" (Bob Seger hit)
26. Golfers' goals
27. Womb mate
28. *Scent of a Woman* star
30. Words with a handshake
32. Cash register
35. Stretches of land
36. Fur trader's item
39. ___ *Doone* (1869 novel)
41. Bausch & ___ (lens maker)

43. Good fortune

44. Pi r squared, for a circle

45. Count (on)

46. Car with a meter

47. *Ben-___* (Heston film)

49. Geese formation

Solution on Page 267

ACROSS

1. Morse code sound
4. TV watchdog: abbr.
7. Word after boom or Bean
11. "Am ___ brother's keeper?"
12. Heidi's mountains
14. Arthur of tennis fame
15. Like hearts and diamonds
16. Opposite of hor.
17. Army food
18. Quake aftershock
20. Astronaut's approval
22. Get on one's nerves
23. ___ salad
27. Copper-zinc alloy
30. Slow-witted
31. ___ Fridays (restaurant chain)
32. Feels lousy
33. Last mo.
34. Fava or lima
35. "I've ___ You Under My Skin"
36. Gen-___ (boomer's kid)
37. The ___ of time
38. Feeds, as a fire
40. Tree with needles
41. MSN, for one
42. Antenna
46. *Les Misérables* author Victor
49. Ken of *thirtysomething*
51. Calendar column: abbr.
52. Headphones cover them
53. In tatters
54. 102, in old Rome
55. *Return of the Jedi* forest dweller
56. Nay negater
57. Elevations: abbr.

DOWN

1. Grime
2. Part of N.A. or S.A.
3. London's ___ Park
4. Party gifts
5. Judge's assistant
6. Short Red Cross course?
7. Carpet fasteners
8. ___Kosh B'Gosh
9. "___ goes there?"
10. Right out of the box
13. Kind of electricity
19. Young lady
21. ___pah band
24. British weapon of WWII
25. Quaint cry of shock
26. Annoying noises
27. Pieces of luggage
28. Read the ___ act
29. One above a tenor
30. German magazine ___ *Spiegel*
33. Tyrant
34. Actress Roseanne

36. Ballot marks

37. "Burnt" crayon color

39. Mall booth

40. Renaissance ___

43. *The Seven Year* ___

44. Take ___ (lose some money)

45. San ___ Obispo, Calif.

46. TV's ___ *Haw*

47. Motor City grp.

48. Miracle-___

50. *The Thin Man* actress

Solution on Page 267

ACROSS

1. ___ Jima
4. Fireplace remnant
7. Point toward
12. Male heir
13. Inc., abroad
14. Big mess
15. Eggs
16. American symbol
18. ___ bender (minor accident)
20. Pack ___ (quit)
21. Senator Hatch
23. Country's McEntire
26. At a tilt
29. Ready-made lawn
30. Continental money unit
31. Spanish day
33. ___ one's loins
34. Suffix with hero
35. Something new in LA?
37. Swedish auto
39. Absolute, as nonsense
40. Study hard and fast
42. Dentists' tools
46. Bridesmaids' counterparts
49. ___ de toilette
50. Taxpayer's dread
51. Sno-cone filler
52. 300 in old Rome
53. Banana skins
54. Hide-hair connector
55. Snickering syllable

DOWN

1. "Time ___ the essence"
2. Used a loom
3. ___ even keel
4. London's Royal ___ Hall
5. Played the lead
6. "Good" cholesterol, briefly
7. At ___ time (prearranged)
8. "...the bombs bursting ___..."
9. Milk of ___ (antacid)
10. CIO partner
11. Early d. of the wk.
17. Kipling's "Gunga ___"
19. "First, ___ harm"
22. ___-proof (easy to operate)
24. Brought into the world
25. Attaches
26. Cinco follower
27. Moon goddess
28. Part of a telephone number
32. Classic retro style
33. Ex–Spice Girl Halliwell
36. Loewe's partner on Broadway
38. Oven setting
39. Speakers' pause fillers
41. Quantities: abbr.
43. Polish Nobelist Walesa

44. Queen Anne's ___

45. ___ as it is

46. Letterman dental feature

47. Wish it weren't so

48. Part of an hr.

Solution on Page 267

ACROSS

1. ___ Piper
5. Bridge unit
9. Japanese "yes"
12. Puerto ___
13. "___ kleine Nachtmusik"
14. Not present: abbr.
15. ___ about (circa)
16. Barn topper
17. "There but for the grace of God ___"
18. Cataract site
20. Phonograph inventor
22. Keep just below a boil
25. Franken and Sharpton
26. All-inclusive
27. Dismiss
30. Hairpiece
31. *Charlotte's Web* author's monogram
33. Four: prefix
37. Nova ___, Canada
40. ___ *Just Not That Into You* (2004 bestseller)
41. Coin flips
42. Colorado trees
45. *20/20* network
46. "___ won't be afraid" ("Stand by Me" lyric)
47. Toward sunrise
49. "No ifs, ___, or buts!"
53. Boy king of ancient Egypt
54. Like EEE shoes
55. *Cheers* actress Perlman
56. NYC clock setting
57. Performed a glissade
58. Knock 'em dead

DOWN

1. Not anti
2. "Boy, am ___ trouble!"
3. Earth-friendly prefix
4. Start of the musical scale
5. Extreme
6. Ms. Zadora
7. Temper, as metal
8. Hider in a haystack
9. Witchy women
10. "Peek-___, I see you!"
11. "Love ___ the Air"
19. "Aw, quit ___ bellyachin'!"
21. Suffix with arbor or arson
22. Emulate Betsy Ross
23. "What's ___ for me?"
24. Homeowner's pymt.
28. Catches on
29. Annual theater award
32. "I ___ only kidding!"
34. Fill in ___ blank
35. Extends a subscription

36. Attack

37. Expressed

38. Corn holder

39. Academy Awards

42. Bettor's starter

43. ___-chef (restaurant assistant)

44. Actor Brad

48. '80s defense prog.

50. Gretzky's org.

51. Anti-narcotics grp.

52. Recite

Solution on Page 268

ACROSS

1. "___ about that!"
4. Bombs that don't explode
8. Hem and ___
11. Graph's x or y
13. "Help ___ the way!"
14. Farrow in films
15. ___ bene
16. Thing you shouldn't do
17. Not normal
18. "___ willikers!"
20. First, second, third, and home
22. Playwright Edward
25. Price
27. AFL's partner
28. Expand
30. "Veni, ___, vici"
34. That female
35. Corporate department
37. Beaver-built barricade
38. Mon. follower
40. Historian's interest
41. "See you later"
42. Former Soviet news agency
44. "Give it ___!"
46. Gently shift to a new topic
49. Victoria's Secret item
50. Co. head
51. When tripled, a WWII movie
54. ___ McAn shoes

58. Alias preceder
59. Lunchtime
60. Having all one's marbles
61. Denver clock setting: abbr.
62. Many NYC dwellings
63. ___ of lamb

DOWN

1. Star Wars pilot Solo
2. Big name in kitchen gadgets
3. Sense of humor
4. Eat well
5. Troop-entertaining grp.
6. ___ *Quixote*
7. Snooty ones
8. Med. care choices
9. Errand runner
10. Rolls of bills
12. Stuffing seasoning
19. Brain scans, briefly
21. Off-road transport, for short
22. German eight
23. "In ___ of flowers…"
24. Make yawn
25. Pepsi and RC
26. Is indebted to
29. Does hip-hop
31. "___ delighted!" ("My pleasure!")
32. Calendar units
33. *How ___ Your Mother* (CBS sitcom)

36. Walk of Fame symbol

39. ___ Sutcliffe, early Beatle

43. Prudential rival

45. Sewer rodents

46. Con artist's art

47. Comic shrieks

48. Capricorn's symbol

49. Makes illegal

52. Caveman Alley

53. Go beyond ripe

55. Actor Holbrook

56. Lowest bill

57. Ryan of *When Harry Met Sally...*

Solution on Page 268

ACROSS

1. Nightwear, briefly
4. "Dancing Queen" quartet
8. Zee preceder
11. Masked critter, for short
13. Scoff
14. Sally Field TV role
15. Cell phone message
16. Civil or elec. expert
17. ___ City Rollers
18. Word on a faucet handle
20. Ex–Mrs. Trump
22. Rodeo rope
25. Alan of *Crimes and Misdemeanors*
27. ___ Beta Kappa
28. Stuffable bread
30. Cartoon frames
34. Pol. party
35. Rise from a chair
37. 12, on a sundial
38. Lhasa ___ (Tibetan dog)
40. Sky color, in Paris
41. Candy in a collectible dispenser
42. Run for it
44. The ones there
46. Takes it easy
49. "Just so you know," on a memo
50. It's scanned at checkout: abbr.
51. Prefix meaning "height"
54. Steffi of tennis
58. ___-jongg (Chinese game)
59. "There's gold in them ___ hills!"
60. Twice tri-
61. Carry on, as a trade
62. Slaw or fries
63. Go by plane

DOWN

1. Agt.'s take
2. Baseball's DiMaggio
3. Chicago White ___
4. "Leaving on ___ Plane"
5. Gentle bear
6. "I ___ your pardon"
7. Right Guard rival
8. Lady hoopsters' org.
9. Chinese currency
10. New Age singer from Ireland
12. Extreme degrees
19. Word from a klutz
21. Rug cleaner, for short
22. Org. for Annika Sorenstam
23. Just ___, skip, and jump away
24. Drinks slowly
25. ___ *of Two Cities*
26. A driver may change one
29. "Can ___ true?"
31. Montreal ballplayer
32. Tells whoppers
33. Petite or jumbo

PUZZLE 43

36. Assigned task
39. Light switch position
43. Exams for future attys.
45. Way up there
46. “One ___ or two?”
47. Down Under gemstone
48. Sore
49. Golfer’s cry
52. Ho ___ Minh
53. “Out of sight!”
55. Gridiron judge
56. Rock’s ___ Rose
57. Wray of *King Kong*

Solution on Page 268

ACROSS

1. Rite Aid competitor
4. "Wait ___!"
8. "That was a long time ___"
11. Miner's tool
13. "You look like you ___ ghost!"
14. Murphy's ___
15. Flight-related prefix
16. Suffix with hip or quip
17. Trio after K
18. Draw ___ in the sand
20. Multiplied by
22. Madison Avenue worker
24. Apprehensive
26. Omaha's home: abbr.
27. Leafy green vegetable
29. Current choice
32. Bird that hoots
33. Moonshine maker
35. "Yoo-___!"
36. Colored, as Easter eggs
38. "You never had ___ good!"
39. Little mischief maker
40. Window covering
42. The British ___
44. Kasparov's game
46. Gave medicine to
48. Animal in a sty
49. Neglect to mention
51. Clapton of rock
54. Mo. before Labor Day
55. Cartoonist Thomas
56. Test driver's car
57. Apr. tax collector
58. Audio feedback problem
59. Complain, complain, complain

DOWN

1. Tax expert, briefly
2. Try (for)
3. Breakfast order
4. Organization: abbr.
5. Cable alternative
6. Mother sheep
7. ___ blanche
8. TV soap opera
9. Checkers or chess
10. Holds the deed to
12. Soft drink nut
19. Squid squirts
21. Gershwin or Levin
22. Give ___ to (acknowledge)
23. Moist, as morning grass
25. Snaky fishes
28. Leave ___ (act gratuitously?)
30. Round roof
31. Police officers
34. Lane of the *Daily Planet*
37. Hosp. workers
41. How two hearts may beat

43. Bit of watermelon waste

44. Spiced tea beverage

45. 1/24 of a day

47. ___ von Bismarck

50. Apple Store buy

52. The Beatles' "___ Loser"

53. Mechanical tooth

Solution on Page 268

ACROSS

1. ___ of Fame
5. Na Na lead-in
8. Former frosh
12. Cleveland's state
13. Football's Dawson
14. Rock band Mötley ___
15. Years and years and years
16. Rearward, at sea
17. "Dear ___"
18. Makes tough
20. Realty parcel
22. *The Taming of the* ___
24. Like some chords: abbr.
27. Oscar or Tony
31. Pizza seasoning
33. Tiny biter
34. Metric weights: abbr.
35. ___ colada (rum cocktail)
36. Flowerlike sea creature
38. Japanese noodles
39. ___ de plume (pen name)
40. Less favorable
42. Opposite of ESE
43. Raises one's glass to
48. Actress Dunaway
51. Premium cable channel
53. Cousin of an onion
54. "___ helpless as a kitten..."
55. Bruins great Bobby
56. Prefix with potent
57. *Peer* ___ (Ibsen play)
58. Twisted, as humor
59. Cotton deseeders

DOWN

1. Clod-busting tools
2. *Cat on* ___ *Tin Roof*
3. Something to draw or toe
4. Get checkmated
5. Cut, as prices
6. Playboy Mansion guy
7. Buck toppers
8. "Shoo, kitty!"
9. Heavenly sphere
10. Place to play darts
11. "You there!"
19. '60s "acid"
21. Have unpaid bills
23. Critic Ebert
24. Disfigure
25. Girl of Green Gables
26. ___ of Arc
27. ___ *for All Seasons*
28. Overindulger of the grape
29. "Lemme ___!" (fightin' words)
30. Sleep phenomenon: abbr.
32. Valedictorian's pride, for short
34. Ability
37. Hold the rights to

1	2	3	4		5	6	7		8	9	10	11
12					13				14			
15					16				17			
18				19			20	21				
				22		23				24	25	26
27	28	29	30			31			32			
33					34				35			
36				37				38				
39				40			41					
			42				43		44	45	46	47
48	49	50			51	52			53			
54					55				56			
57					58				59			

38. ___ Speedwagon (1970s–'80s band)

41. Tale

42. Toward the sunset

44. Easy as falling off ___

45. Rig on the road

46. Where Nashville is: abbr.

47. Downhill aids

48. Mediterranean fruit

49. First daughter Carter

50. ___ Can Cook (former cooking show)

52. "Man, it's cold!"

Solution on Page 269

ACROSS

1. Pre-stereo sound
5. Plastic pipe material
8. Goodies for gala attendees
12. Get the wrinkles out
13. Fireworks reaction
14. Make money
15. Try to locate
16. Prefix with light or night
17. Paul who sang "Puppy Love"
18. "Holy" Ohio town
20. Bottommost
22. "Tasty!"
23. Easter egg coating
24. *Sesame Street* network
27. Former veep Quayle
29. Gives for a time
33. Thailand, formerly
35. Rather's network
37. Rock's ___ Straits
38. Dental filling
40. Middle: abbr.
42. W's successors?
43. Arcing shot
45. Oxcart's track
47. Capital of Minnesota
50. Alphas' opposites
54. ___ sci (college major, informally)
55. Flash drive port
57. Biblical gift bearers
58. What modest people lack
59. Bring to court
60. Outlet insert
61. Walk in shallow water
62. Aaron's 755: abbr.
63. Archie or Jughead

DOWN

1. *Gorillas in the* ___
2. Cookie with a creamy middle
3. Yuletide song
4. Perfectly pitched
5. Washington's river
6. Solemn promise
7. Youngster
8. Sushi wrap
9. Wax's opposite
10. Clumsy boats
11. Pesky flying insect
19. Defective firecracker
21. Olive in the comics
24. Pitchfork-shaped Greek letter
25. Coal holder
26. Actor Mineo
28. *The West Wing* network
30. Put the kibosh on
31. Moistureless
32. "Oh yeah? ___ who?"
34. The blahs
36. Flashing lights

39. Last word of the golden rule

41. ___ and Coke (mixed drink)

44. Turn red from embarrassment

46. Entice

47. Eject, as lava

48. Draped attire

49. Trudge along

51. Battering wind

52. Flulike symptoms

53. Aries or Libra

56. California's Big ___

Solution on Page 269

ACROSS

1. Edmonton hockey player
6. Recyclables container
9. Curve in the road
12. Japanese cartoon art genre
13. "This ___ stickup!"
14. Key near the space bar
15. Mind reading
17. *The Facts of Life* actress Charlotte
18. String after Q
19. "Ho ho ho" crier
21. Pre-calc course
24. Three ___ kind
27. More than want
28. Baseball's Doubleday
30. Congregational cries
32. Deep hole
33. "It's ___ a day's work"
35. Price label
38. Mythical underworld
40. ~
42. What the "ten" of "hang ten" refers to
44. Justice Dept. division
46. Wall Street abbr.
47. Perfect school grade
49. Massachusetts cape
51. Lion constellation
52. Desperate, as an effort
58. ___-Magnon
59. "Leaving ___ Jet Plane"
60. Get-up-and-go
61. Maple tree fluid
62. Lucky rabbit's foot, e.g.
63. Likely to talk back

DOWN

1. Grain in granola
2. Suffix with serpent
3. Rapper ___ Wayne
4. Exit one's cocoon
5. Exerciser's sets
6. Bridle part
7. Suffix with devil
8. Votes against
9. With deep sincerity
10. Blackboard material
11. Stand in good ___
16. From point ___ point B
20. Late columnist Landers
21. Keg opening
22. Slugger's stat
23. Privy to confidential information
25. Not true
26. "What ___, a mind reader?"
29. "Way cool!"
31. Sinus doc
34. Fluorescent bulb alternative, for short
36. Circulars, basically
37. "I didn't know that!"

39. Sun Devils' sch.
41. Prime Minister Gandhi
42. Bathroom powders
43. *The Magic Flute*, for one
45. Broadway play segment
48. Hog's food
50. Gambler's numbers

53. "Gimme ___!" (Alabama cheerleader's cry)
54. Wood-cutting tool
55. Opposite of 'tain't
56. Walgreens rival
57. "___ Jude" (Beatles classic)

Solution on Page 269

ACROSS

1. Spaghetti or ziti
6. Take a siesta
9. Prefix with life or wife
12. Like one of the two jaws
13. *The King and I* star Brynner
14. End of some email addresses
15. Light refractor
16. One learning the ropes
18. Kublai ___
20. Once a year
21. Middling grade
23. Hangmen's ropes
25. North Carolina's capital
27. Subject
31. Served perfectly, in tennis
32. Rowing blade
34. Songstress Horne
35. His and her
37. Closes again, as an envelope
39. Beefsteak or cherry
41. Stadium cry
42. "Tennis, ___?"
45. Air passage
47. 3-D art project
49. Harder to find
52. Director Lee
53. Online "ha-ha"
54. Nail file material
55. It follows April in Paris
56. High-speed connection, for short
57. Plow maker John

DOWN

1. Young seal
2. Busy mo. at the IRS
3. *Malcolm X* director
4. New Age composer John
5. Fashion designer Giorgio
6. *WSJ* alternative
7. Surrounding glows
8. Mercury or Mars
9. Bill of fare
10. Bright thought
11. Sword fight, e.g.
17. Shoe cushion
19. Like a scrubbed space mission
21. Suffix with techno-
22. Per unit
24. Scarlett of *Gone with the Wind*
26. Film cutter
28. Partridge's perch, in song
29. *To Live and Die* ___
30. Money in a wallet
33. On a pension: abbr.
36. President Reagan
38. Turned bad, as milk
40. Interoffice notes
42. Comic Sandler
43. One of Columbus's ships

44. Jellystone Park denizen

46. "And it ____ to pass…"

48. Jack-of-____-trades

50. Make a miscue

51. Corned beef sandwich bread

Solution on Page 269

ACROSS

1. Tavern
4. Rocket launch site
7. Prepares to shoot
11. Fuel economy org.
12. "Movin' ___" (*The Jeffersons* theme song)
14. Layer of paint
15. Poverty-stricken
17. Rumple, as hair
18. Wanting
19. "Ready when you ___!"
21. Caustic substance
22. Out of one's mind
26. "Say cheese!"
29. Leaky tire sound
30. Blend
31. At a ___ for words
32. "The Tell-Tale Heart" author
33. Running speed
34. Large coffeepot
35. Developer's site
36. Assistants
37. Command before "Go!"
39. Suffix with hobby or lobby
40. ___ kwon do
41. Horse house
45. "Top ___ mornin'!"
48. Biblical vessel
50. Gather what's been sown
51. Airport conveyance
52. Average guy
53. Rowan and Marino
54. "His Master's Voice" co.
55. "___ another thing…"

DOWN

1. Mani-___
2. Words before arms or smoke
3. Building near a silo
4. Spinach-eating sailor
5. Battery terminal
6. Simon and Garfunkel, e.g.
7. Highest points
8. Promise of payment
9. Rainey and Barker
10. Kin of aves.
13. Heap kudos on
16. Spills the beans
20. D's associates
23. Make ___ dash for
24. Pleasing
25. Donald and Ivana, e.g.
26. Fake coin
27. Additional amount
28. "___ it a pity?"
29. Drunkard
32. Powerful
33. Breads with pockets
35. Grazing ground

PUZZLE 49

36. Respiratory disorder
38. Stair parts
39. Sci-fi writer Asimov
42. Mexican peninsula
43. Scientologist Hubbard
44. ___ out a living (barely got by)
45. Fort ___, Calif.
46. Earl Grey or oolong
47. Solo of Star Wars
49. Hockey legend Bobby

Solution on Page 270

ACROSS

1. Bamboozle
5. When repeated, a ballroom dance
8. Rushmore and Rainier: abbr.
11. Tennis score after deuce
12. Univ. offering
13. Handle roughly
14. Oodles
15. W-2 ID
16. Word form for "eight"
17. Black cattle breed
19. Hemingway or Borgnine
21. Engine speed, for short
23. Teeny
24. Led down the aisle
28. Up ___ (cornered)
32. Calypso cousin
33. Comedian DeLuise
35. "To thine ___ self be true"
36. Locations
39. Infused with oxygen
42. Rock's ___ Lobos
44. Linden of *Barney Miller*
45. "Semper fi" guy
48. ___ four (teacake)
52. Tell it like ___
53. Friend of Fidel
56. ___ Hashanah
57. Seating section
58. Restaurant bill
59. *Newsweek* rival
60. Scale units: abbr.
61. Family member
62. ___ to stern

DOWN

1. Computer input or output
2. Thick Japanese noodle
3. Sonar sound
4. Safeguard
5. PC inserts
6. Men and boys
7. Nixon's first veep
8. Riot spray
9. King ___ tomb
10. One-armed bandit, briefly
13. Water Lilies painter Claude
18. Apr. season
20. Actor Stephen
22. Pre-___ student
24. Capt. Kirk's ___ *Enterprise*
25. Go downhill fast
26. Head covering
27. ___ good deed
29. Start to smell, maybe
30. Ram's ma'am
31. Bring to a conclusion
34. Verbal shrug
37. Beethoven's "Für ___"
38. ___ of a gun

40. Hit on the knuckles
41. Warns
43. Religious splinter groups
45. Pepper grinder
46. Get from ___ (progress slightly)
47. Fixes, as a fight

49. "There's nothing ___!" ("Easy!")
50. "Woe ___!"
51. "It's us against ___"
54. "Bali ___" (*South Pacific* song)
55. Go out, like the tide

Solution on Page 270

ACROSS

1. Tiebreakers, briefly
4. ___ Good Men
8. Totally absorbed (in)
12. Army bed
13. El ___ (Pacific phenomenon)
14. One who's on your side
15. New Deal proj.
16. "Whip It" rock group
17. Small container for liquids
18. Winnebagos, briefly
20. Sheep's coat
22. They "speak louder than words"
26. Ed of The Mary Tyler Moore Show
27. Soothing ointment
28. Strong as ___
30. B–F connection
31. Backwoods refusal
32. From A ___
35. Remedy
36. À la ___ (with ice cream)
37. Conversation starter
41. Fencing call
43. Is of use to
45. Jump on one foot
46. Have ___ on (claim)
47. Cry of woe
50. D–H connection
53. Semi-convertible auto roof
54. Gehrig and Costello
55. Sheriff's asst.
56. Rowboat propellers
57. By ___ of (owing to)
58. Wt. units

DOWN

1. Pumpkin-carving mo.
2. "Mazel ___!"
3. Scare suddenly
4. "___ it goes"
5. Old expression of disgust
6. Ltr. container
7. Canine sound
8. Great reviews
9. Visitor from another planet
10. Location
11. "Tippecanoe and ___ too"
19. Energy
21. Hardly strict
22. Alphabet openers
23. Real heel
24. Half of Mork's farewell
25. Rimshot instrument
29. Wilson of The Royal Tenenbaums
32. Underwater missile
33. Unmatched, as a sock
34. Last letter
35. Row's opp.
36. Onetime Chinese chairman
37. "If I ___ do it all over again…"

38. "Don't Cry for Me Argentina" musical
39. Toil
40. Calls a spade a thpade
42. Apparition
44. Auctioned off
48. ___ polloi (commoners)
49. Mother Teresa, for one
51. Turk's topper
52. Certain MDs

Solution on Page 270

ACROSS

1. Give birth to
6. ___ B. Anthony
11. Singer Nicks of Fleetwood Mac
12. Sanctuary
14. Fold, as paper
15. City with canals
16. What we breathe
17. Borders
19. "Don't Bring Me Down" band
20. Winnebago owner, for short
22. ___ Vegas
23. Hot off the presses
24. Tranquilizes
26. On a need-to-know ___
28. Ring victories, briefly
29. Get ___ of (throw away)
30. What some crooks crack
33. Soloist's showcase
37. When doubled, an African fly
38. Ring rock
39. "I never ___ man I didn't like" (Will Rogers)
40. Like an antique
41. Start to wilt
43. "Smoking or ___?"
44. "But will it play in ___?"
46. Money back
48. One thing after another
49. Entraps
50. Jeans and khakis
51. Brought to a conclusion

DOWN

1. Try hard
2. Squinted
3. Screen siren Gardner
4. Sensible
5. Christmas tree shedding
6. Puts aside
7. Utilizes
8. Roget wd.
9. Martians and such
10. Cell centers
11. Marks for life
13. Cat calls
18. Car fuel
21. ___ over the coals
25. How-___ (instructional books)
26. Lighter and pen maker
27. Take ___ view of (frown on)
29. Regret
30. Comes to an end
31. Snoozing
32. Felt hat
33. Classic auto
34. Professor's security blanket
35. Made amends
36. Touches down
38. Whitman's *Leaves of* ___

41. Weight-loss program

42. *Dead Man Walking* star Sean

45. ___ Tin Tin (TV dog)

47. It's all the rage

Solution on Page 270

ACROSS

1. Choose (to)
4. "Me, myself, ___"
8. Aviated
12. Not against
13. Greenish blue
14. Sitarist Shankar
15. Winter bug
16. Turner and Danson
17. One taking a gander
18. "___ evil, hear…"
20. Not tidy
21. Sheathe
25. Box-office flop
28. Litter weakling
29. Radar gun meas.
32. Blossom-to-be
33. Smidgens
34. Life story, for short
35. Gal. divisions
36. Absconded with
37. Backfire sound
38. Remove from office
40. Fastening device
44. Glaringly vivid
48. Disrespectful
49. Demolish, as a building
52. Australian bird with rudimentary wings
53. "That's ___ blow!"
54. Corporate bigwig, for short
55. Response: abbr.
56. Pesters
57. TV rooms
58. Bon ___ (witty remark)

DOWN

1. Slays, mob-style
2. ___ vault
3. Factual
4. Follow, as advice
5. TV's Science Guy Bill
6. "Dear old" fellow
7. Write-___ (some votes)
8. On the house
9. ___ into (attacks)
10. Pre-holiday nights
11. Lean and muscular
19. Cornhusker St.
20. 2000 Subway Series losers
22. Sing like Bing
23. Cars
24. Anaconda, e.g.
25. Cookout, briefly
26. ___ to lunch
27. RNs' coworkers
29. Wharton deg.
30. Bowling target
31. Greedy type
33. Whoop ___ (celebrate)

37. Heat measure: abbr.

39. Baldwin and Guinness

40. Maryland seafood specialty

41. Little ___ of the comics

42. Work like ___

43. Kitten cries

45. Quantity of paper

46. "___ expert, but…"

47. Do housework

49. Ketchup-colored

50. Wood-chopping tool

51. Kind of Buddhism

Solution on Page 271

ACROSS

1. +
5. Big Bird's network
8. Bungle
12. Author Austen
13. Encouragement for a matador
14. Old-time wisdom
15. X may mark it
16. "Walk, don't ___!"
17. "Heads ___, tails…"
18. Small child
20. Peak of a wave
21. Argentina neighbor
24. Take ___ the waist (tailor's job)
26. Apportions, with "out"
27. "___ if I can help it!"
28. Not Dem. or Rep.
31. Mantra sounds
32. Inc., in England
33. Benjamin Hoff's *The ___ of Pooh*
34. Govt. code crackers
35. "Phooey!"
36. 1965 Alabama march site
38. London's ___ Gallery
39. Wheel rods
40. Secret messages
43. Lose color
45. Door-to-door cosmetics seller
46. Rand McNally product
47. Shed, as skin

51. ___-to-riches
52. Prefix with sphere or system
53. Winnie-the-___
54. "You're something ___!"
55. "With this ring, I thee ___"
56. "And miles ___ before I sleep"

DOWN

1. Bedwear, briefly
2. Full circle, on the track
3. "One," in Madrid
4. Come to terms
5. "The other white meat"
6. Extremely exasperated
7. 1 of 100 in DC
8. Play the coquette
9. *St. Elmo's Fire* actor Rob
10. Author Leon
11. Not straight
19. "That's correct"
20. Lion or tiger
21. "Let's go!"
22. ___ and haws
23. ___ *Wonderful Life*
25. Sign of approval
28. "___ be over soon"
29. It's given to a newborn
30. "When in Rome, ___ the Romans…"
32. Back muscle, briefly

35. Some coll. degrees
36. Sorrowful
37. Free (from)
38. Past, present, or future
40. Part of c/o
41. The White House's ___ Office
42. Canines

44. Like two peas in ___
46. Kitten call
48. Tic-tac-toe victory
49. Captain's record
50. Even if, informally

Solution on Page 271

ACROSS

1. ___-Hartley Act
5. Author Rand
8. Display
12. Lyft alternative
13. One of the Stooges
14. Hatcher or Garr
15. Repetitive learning method
16. Psalms follower
18. Olympic skating medalist Michelle
19. Be acquainted with
20. Made a hole
23. Windowsill
27. Frog's perch
31. "Durn it!"
32. $20 bill dispenser, briefly
33. Burst of growth
36. Coffee holder
37. Breathe rapidly
39. French composer Claude
41. Walk through puddles
43. Moving truck
44. Record player
47. Cereal in party mix
51. Mischance
55. Baby sheep
56. Serve coffee
57. ___ Balls: Hostess snacks
58. Googly-eyed Muppet
59. It goes with a nut
60. Scatter, as seeds
61. "Come Sail Away" band

DOWN

1. Istanbul native
2. Take ___ (acknowledge applause)
3. Cheese in a Greek salad
4. Hip
5. Unit of elec. current
6. Part of NYC
7. Advertising sign gas
8. Drunk as a skunk
9. ___ Majesty the Queen
10. Spherical body
11. The Badger St.
17. Tennessee athlete, for short
21. FedEx rival
22. Opening
24. Beavers' constructions
25. African antelopes
26. Like omelets
27. Trips around the track
28. Slanted type: abbr.
29. K–P connection
30. Bad firecracker
34. Gun the engine
35. "We'll let you know," on a TV schedule
38. "All I got was this lousy ___"
40. Dad's brothers

42. Put out of sight

45. ___ up (come clean)

46. ___ time (quickly)

48. Sentry's "Stop!"

49. TV award

50. Microsoft game system

51. Police dept. alert

52. Pigeon's sound

53. ___-de-sac (blind alley)

54. Aid for a stranded auto

Solution on Page 271

ACROSS

1. Air traffic control agcy.
4. Escalator segment
8. Foreshadow
12. Belly muscles, for short
13. Dance done in grass skirts
14. Off-base, unofficially
15. Soup order
16. Having ___ hair day
17. Musical symbol
18. PC key
19. *Star* ___ (Shatner show)
21. Blue-green hue
23. Banana waste
24. Women's ___
27. Levin and Gershwin
29. ___ *It to Beaver*
31. Evening meal
34. Judged
35. Revises, as text
36. Neighbor of Mass.
37. Corn on the ___
38. ___ Grey tea
40. When tripled, a *Seinfeld* catchphrase
44. Give up, as rights
45. Tree with cones
46. Easy as falling ___ log
49. Partners of aahs
52. Adolescent boy
53. Naysayers' words
54. Ballerina's bend
55. "It's ___-brainer!"
56. Blubbers
57. Short-term worker
58. It runs on the road

DOWN

1. Diamond surface
2. Mistreat
3. Pet-protecting org.
4. TV's ___ *Na Na*
5. Bath site
6. Makes very happy
7. Mission priest
8. Supply with funding
9. Hooter
10. Anonymous John
11. Santa helper
20. Funny DeGeneres
22. Fabric fluff
23. 72, at Pebble Beach
24. On the ___ (fleeing)
25. "___ Been Working on the Railroad"
26. Bon Jovi's "___ of Roses"
28. View again
30. Start of a counting-out rhyme
31. Christmas mo.
32. Bride's declaration
33. Tip of a pen

34. Amer. currency

36. Louisiana language

39. Take as one's own

41. Insurance giant with a spokesduck

42. Ross of the Supremes

43. Passion

44. Mama of The Mamas & the Papas

46. Carry-___ (small pieces of luggage)

47. Egg ___ yung

48. Leap day's mo.

50. That guy

51. Fall mo.

Solution on Page 271

ACROSS

1. Prefix with skirt or series
5. Gene material, in brief
8. Toast topper
11. The end ___ era
12. Make dirty
13. Breakfast drinks, for short
14. Have a yen for
15. Proofreader's find
16. Show the effects of weight
17. Less fresh
19. Makes irate
21. Lipton rival
23. Lopsided, as a grin
26. Understand, as a joke
27. Ewes' mates
31. "I'm Gonna Wash That Man Right ___ My Hair"
33. Sock front
35. Dullsville
36. Marries
37. Timothy Leary's drug
39. Be inquisitive
40. Mother ___
43. Think highly of
46. Lend a hand
51. Mauna ___
52. Left Turn ___ (street sign)
54. Mafia boss
55. Sgt.'s superiors
56. ___ ex machina
57. In the center of
58. Library admonition
59. Brain scan, for short
60. Western alliance, for short

DOWN

1. Cuts the grass
2. "___ first you don't succeed…"
3. Grandmother, affectionately
4. Worldwide: abbr.
5. Orbison who sang "Only the Lonely"
6. Try to bite, puppy-style
7. On one's own
8. Canseco of baseball
9. Opened just a crack
10. Txts, e.g.
12. *Sesame* ___
18. Neighbor of Scot.
20. Clothing
22. Mink wrap
23. "Unbelievable!"
24. Golden Girl MacClanahan
25. From Jan. 1 until now, in accounting
28. Austrian peak
29. Deface
30. Wallflowerish
32. Spumante city
34. School papers

124

38. Karl Marx's ___ *Kapital*

41. Gradually wear away

42. Actress Zellweger

43. "___ fair in love…"

44. "The lady ___ protest too much" (*Hamlet*)

45. Prepare potatoes, in a way

47. Make a digital image of

48. "Today ___ man" (bar mitzvah declaration)

49. Roasting rod

50. Heading for a chore list

53. Big galoot

Solution on Page 272

ACROSS

1. "Be Prepared" org.
4. Participate in a bee
9. Director Brooks
12. Part of TGIF
13. Threepio's buddy
14. Sailor's assent
15. Physician's nickname
16. ___ game (pitcher's dream)
17. Driving range barrier
18. Dubai dignitary
20. Tightened
22. *Der* ___ (German magazine)
24. Allergy symptom
27. That guy's
28. Jenny Craig client
30. State with confidence
33. Roasts' hosts
34. Makes off with
35. "Stop the cameras!"
36. Formal agreement
37. Weapons stash
41. In working order
44. Explorer of kids' TV
45. Galahad's title
47. Irreligious one
49. Twain's talent
50. Valedictorian's rank
51. Fatter than fat
52. Faith Hill's "Take Me ___ Am"

53. HP products
54. Peeled
55. Kyoto currency

DOWN

1. ___ one's time (waits)
2. Put one's foot down
3. Computer text can be written in this
4. ___ Andreas fault
5. Campus sit-ins
6. Lucy's landlady
7. Butcher's cut
8. Land parcels
9. Authoritative order
10. Bird's-___ view
11. "___ there be light"
19. Warms up, as leftovers
21. Put together
23. Young lady
25. Observe
26. 60-min. periods
28. Lessen
29. Don of talk radio
30. Egyptian serpent
31. RR stop
32. Makes safe
37. Rags-to-riches author
38. "Impossible!"
39. Pop up

1	2	3		4	5	6	7	8		9	10	11
12				13						14		
15				16						17		
18			19		20				21			
22				23					24		25	26
			27				28	29				
30	31	32					33					
34							35					
36						37				38	39	40
		41		42	43				44			
45	46			47				48		49		
50				51						52		
53				54						55		

40. Language of ancient Rome

42. Individually

43. Ali who said "Open sesame!"

45. Apply bread to gravy

46. *Monsters,* ___ (2001 Pixar film)

48. Beatty of *Deliverance*

Solution on Page 272

ACROSS

1. Singer Celine
5. Bundle of cotton
9. CD spinners
12. "Leggo my ___!"
13. Was beholden to
14. Yahoo! alternative
15. Microbe
16. Donations for the poor
17. "I Like ___" ('50s political slogan)
18. Precipitous
20. Reduced, as pain
22. Plays for time
26. Govt. media watchdog
29. "Skip ___ Lou"
30. "Lions and tigers and bears" follower
34. Snobs put them on
36. *Car Talk* network
37. Phobia
38. Part of NFL: abbr.
39. Sheer delight
41. Ozs. and lbs.
42. Dwell (on)
44. Sheriff's star
47. Hitchhiker's digit
52. *The Simpsons* storekeeper
53. Discover
57. Drive-___ window
58. Physique, informally
59. Expression of understanding
60. ___ the line (obeyed)
61. Computer filename extension
62. Helen of ___
63. Advanced degrees

DOWN

1. BA and BS, e.g.
2. "___ a Kick Out of You"
3. Folklore meany
4. City on Seward Peninsula
5. Breathtaking snake
6. Piercing tool
7. Moon vehicle, for short
8. '50s Ford failure
9. Speaker's platform
10. Wisecrack
11. Iditarod transport
19. Winter hrs. in L.A.
21. Beginning on
23. Ice grabbers
24. More than sufficient
25. Ancient stringed instruments
26. Devotee
27. US spy org.
28. PC screen
31. Use an ax
32. Yoga class surface
33. 12-mo. periods
35. Trudge through the mire

40. More than -er

43. Suit well

44. Baseball great Ruth

45. "___ on both your houses!"

46. ___, *Where's My Car?* (2000 comedy)

48. Website address starter

49. "Now we're in trouble!"

50. TV talking horse

51. Flowers-to-be

54. Jerusalem is its cap.

55. Prefix with natal or classical

56. *L.A. Law* actress

Solution on Page 272

ACROSS

1. Gloppy stuff
4. Roll up, as a sail
8. Hooligan
12. Red Roof ___
13. "Just the Two ___"
14. Hades
15. Communications conglomerate
16. Capital of Italia
17. Peruvian of yore
18. Producer's dream
20. In layers
22. "I'll be right there!"
25. Flaming
26. Motion picture
27. Abbr. on a memo
30. Tanning lotion abbr.
31. Hostile force
32. Angler's pole
35. Anti-fur org.
36. ___-nine-tails
37. "___ tell you something…"
41. Do needlework
43. Off the mark
45. State east of Wash.
46. Eight on a sundial
47. "Q ___ queen"
50. Prefix for light
53. *Silent Spring* subj.
54. Trim, as costs
55. Relieved sounds
56. Scottish miss
57. Fraternal group
58. Go one better than

DOWN

1. Musician's engagement
2. Toronto's prov.
3. Two quarters
4. Strong suit
5. Flying saucer
6. Daiquiri base
7. Future attorney's exam: abbr.
8. Burglar
9. Painter Matisse
10. Painful stomach problem
11. Air freshener brand
19. School of thought
21. Fleming who created 007
22. Suppositions
23. Puppy's bite
24. Sidewalk eatery
28. Diaper wearer
29. Lipton products
32. Machine gun sound
33. AMEX alternative
34. Homer Simpson exclamation
35. Pig's digs
36. El ___ (Heston role)
37. Tool with a bubble

38. *Fear of Fifty* writer Jong

39. Sextet halves

40. Sends out

42. Fork prongs

44. Gift-wrapping need

48. Mineo of *Exodus*

49. Vex

51. Owl's question?

52. AOL, for one

Solution on Page 272

ACROSS

1. *Wheel of Fortune* action
5. Sun emanations
9. Pen contents
12. Citrus flavor
13. Newspaper notice
14. Be litigious
15. "For" votes
16. Mimicking bird
17. Former C&W station
18. "Nearer, My God, to ___"
20. A dozen dozen
22. Moon stage
25. ___ rule (normally)
26. Dorm monitors: abbr.
27. Throw ___ (get angry)
30. Get an eyeful
34. Large deer
35. Wanders
37. Switz. neighbor
38. Close, as an envelope
40. "___ Lonesome I Could Cry"
41. Geller who claims paranormal ability
42. 180 degrees from WNW
44. Fee schedule
46. Biblical tower site
49. Throat-clearer's sound
51. Buckeyes' sch.
52. Thomas ___ Edison
54. Doctrines
58. "Un momento, ___ favor"
59. Cowboy's footwear
60. Narrow cut
61. Live from NY show
62. Scatters, as seed
63. Grasp

DOWN

1. Crafty
2. ___ à la mode
3. John Denver's "Thank God ___ Country Boy"
4. Wasps' homes
5. *Gladiator* setting
6. "Rock-___ Baby"
7. Yang's counterpart
8. Male deer
9. "What ___ become of me?"
10. Women in habits
11. Some male dolls
19. *See No Evil, ___ No Evil* (1989)
21. Use for an old T-shirt
22. Oval Office occupant, briefly
23. ___ and hearty
24. "May I ___ favor?"
25. $20 bill dispensers
28. Pâté de ___ gras
29. "___ Woman" (Reddy song)
31. Bust ___ (laugh hard)
32. "___ all in this together"

33. ___ Kringle

36. Like bad losers

39. *Mo' Better Blues* director Spike

43. Thick chunks

45. Some Pennsylvania Dutch

46. Conks on the head

47. "Well, I'll be ___ of a gun!"

48. Singer Ives

49. State openly

50. Milliner's supply

53. London lavatory

55. ___-mo replay

56. $1,000,000, for short

57. Part of EST

Solution on Page 273

ACROSS

1. Escargot
6. Cube with 21 dots
9. WSW's reverse
12. Reddish hair dye
13. Mighty long time
14. Letter after cee
15. Praise highly
16. Singer DiFranco
17. ___ *Haw*
18. Heaven's gatekeeper
20. College transcript no.
22. "Go, ___!"
23. Country singer Haggard
26. Guitar cousin
29. "Calm down!"
31. Summer shoe
34. Saint Francis of ___
35. Heavenly
37. Kangaroo pouch
38. Celebrity skewering
39. "Buenos ___"
42. Zero
43. Welsh ___ (cheesy dish)
47. Middle X of X-X-X
49. Brian of ambient music
51. Schiller's "___ Joy"
52. Mine output
53. ___ Lanka
54. Beauty parlor

55. Prefix with "understanding"
56. Pre-coll. exam
57. Diary passage, e.g.

DOWN

1. Spike Lee's ___ *Gotta Have It*
2. Adjacent (to)
3. Take ___ (snooze)
4. Cove
5. Caffè with hot milk
6. "Oh, what am I to do?"
7. Electrically charged atom
8. Mysteries
9. John Glenn portrayer in *The Right Stuff*
10. Word before a maiden name
11. Extra-wide, on a shoebox
19. Bird on the Great Seal of the United States
21. Cribbage pieces
24. Bart Simpson's sister
25. Of sweeping proportions
26. ___-friendly
27. Green Hornet's sidekick
28. Improves
30. Actress Shire of *Rocky*
32. Lucy's husband
33. Unsophisticated
36. Dexterous
40. Got out of bed

134

41. Four-door car

44. Alternative to suspenders

45. "Like ___ not…"

46. Crooner Bennett

47. Novelist Clancy

48. Onassis who married Jackie

50. Org. that champions Second Amendment rights

Solution on Page 273

ACROSS

1. "___ the word!"
5. Quite impressed
9. Body art, for short
12. Oil cartel
13. PBS science program
14. Pigs out (on), briefly
15. Ark unit
16. Sign of sorrow
18. American flag feature
20. Hair removal brand
21. Novelist Simpson
23. Bread unit
26. Hang
29. Share and share ___
30. Marlene Dietrich's "___ Bin Die Fesche Lola"
31. Makes docile
33. Mom, to Auntie
34. Dental thread
36. Renowned
38. "I ___ I taw a puddy…"
39. Naked
40. Sidewalk border
43. ___ *Weapon* (Mel Gibson film)
47. Hawkeye Pierce portrayer
50. Trillion: prefix
51. ___ and don'ts
52. Business attire
53. Shower with praise
54. "Give the devil his ___"
55. Baseball's Rose
56. Jittery

DOWN

1. Cleans the floor
2. ___ the crack of dawn
3. Israel's Golda
4. Pinch pennies
5. Pre-cable need
6. Tale of ___
7. Sen. Bayh of Indiana
8. Madonna's *Truth or* ___
9. Hare racer
10. Needless fuss
11. Medicinal amt.
17. Farmer's hangout, in a children's song
19. *Dead* ___ *Society*
22. Madison Avenue types
24. Closely related (to)
25. Gab or song ending
26. Refine, as flour
27. Campus near Beverly Hills, briefly
28. Put in the spotlight
29. "All joking ___…"
32. Act like
35. Leave speechless
37. Prickly plant
41. Throaty utterance

42. Like a clear sky

44. Noggin

45. Snug as a bug in ___

46. ___ Gaga

47. Calculate column totals

48. Mary's TV boss

49. Morse code word

Solution on Page 273

ACROSS

1. Lower leg
5. Highways: abbr.
8. Pro ___ (like some legal work)
12. Corn syrup brand
13. Lemon or lime drink
14. Many a Mideasterner
15. "Take ___ face value"
16. Golf ball's perch
17. Scroogean outbursts
18. Thickheaded
20. ER workers
22. Run out, as a subscription
25. Cut the lawn
28. California peak
31. Absurd comedy
33. Co. honchos
34. "La la" preceder
36. Small pieces
37. Hawaiian hi
39. Emphasize
41. PBJ alternative
42. Toward the back
44. It breaks the silence of the lambs
45. "Git!"
50. Beep with a beeper
53. Gateway Arch city: abbr.
56. Snake dancers of the Southwest
57. Hertz rival
58. Singer Zadora
59. Stunt legend Knievel
60. Already in the mail
61. Fix a button, say
62. On the ___ (recuperating)

DOWN

1. Lose traction
2. Loathe
3. Tehran's nation
4. Forget-me-___
5. Squealer
6. He followed HST
7. Watermelon throwaways
8. Streisand nickname
9. "…cup ___ cone?"
10. "I'd rather not"
11. Out of date: abbr.
19. Followers of kays
21. Ump's relative
23. Letters on a telephone bill
24. Dissect grammatically
25. Some med. scans
26. Halloween mos.
27. Filmmaker Craven
28. Trader's option
29. Owl sound
30. Fireplace remains
32. Lincoln, familiarly
33. Taxi
35. One ___ time (singly)

138

PUZZLE 64

38. Roadside assistance org.

40. Train lines: abbr.

43. Talks hoarsely

44. Crème de la crème

46. High school sci. course

47. Wander about

48. With the stroke of ___

49. Not spicy

50. Partners for mas

51. Pennsylvania or Madison: abbr.

52. Tonic go-with

54. Make equal, as the score

55. Perry Mason's field

Solution on Page 273

ACROSS

1. Uncertain
5. Word of advice
8. Sink's alternative
12. Whodunit board game
13. UCLA rival
14. *The ___ 'Clock News*
15. Hawaiian coffee region
16. "Thanks, ___ no thanks"
17. Decorate again
18. Give this for that
20. Radioactive gas
21. Ship of Columbus
24. Boeing 747, e.g.
25. Up to one's ears
26. Purple flowers
29. Clean the floor
30. Pot-bellied critter
31. Collagen injection site
33. Fitted one within another
36. Africa's Sierra ___
38. At once
39. Uneasy feeling
40. Hatfield adversary
43. Sits in (for)
45. Diamond Head's island
46. Hesitation sounds
47. Kids' guessing game
51. Shutter strip
52. Kind of pie
53. Karmann ___ (old Volkswagen)
54. Not his
55. Tiger Woods's grp.
56. Part of a bottle

DOWN

1. "Ugh!"
2. Mel's Diner waitress
3. Enjoyment
4. They raise dough
5. Big brass instrument
6. "The jig ___!"
7. Mtge. point, for example
8. Rock layers
9. Garden invader
10. Prefix with European or China
11. *Apollo 11* destination
19. Baby's bawl
20. Meth. or Cath.
21. Popular cooking spray
22. Victor's cry
23. Place for a necklace clasp
24. Lively Irish dance
26. Blow the ___ off (expose)
27. Heavy shoe
28. Transgressions
30. Church seat
32. Four-footed friend
34. Pig noses
35. Cracker Jack bonus

36. Scientific workplace

37. Junior naval officer

40. ___ pit (rock concert area)

41. Race driver Yarborough

42. Blacken on the grill

43. Self-satisfied

44. Fed. food inspectors

46. Strike caller

48. "There ___ Is, Miss America"

49. Snapshot, for short

50. Chatter

Solution on Page 274

ACROSS

1. Minks and sables
5. Billy Joel's "___ to Extremes"
8. Pitch black
12. Get ___ a good thing
13. Chaney of horror films
14. Delany of *China Beach*
15. Religious ceremony
16. Vinyl records
17. *CHiPs* star Estrada
18. Breathe out
20. Passes, as a law
22. Three ___ Night
23. Actor Robbins
24. Wine descriptor
27. Awful
29. Puts up, as a painting
33. Goes kaput
35. Commit perjury
37. "...borrower ___ lender be"
38. Pole carving
40. UK leaders
42. Gender
43. Ultimate degree
45. Bridge action
47. Salad leaf
50. Unable to agree
54. Roman tyrant
55. Gretzky's grp.
57. Theater chain founder Marcus
58. Wed. follower
59. Summa ___ laude
60. Pound of literature
61. Edges
62. Bad ___ (German spa)
63. Reject, as an accusation

DOWN

1. Cannoneer's command
2. Operating system developed at Bell Labs
3. IRA variety
4. Three-time Masters winner Sam
5. Prohibited
6. Elephant's org.
7. Beginning stage
8. Creative guy
9. Antidrug cop
10. Work with yarn
11. Tibetan beasts
19. Soft toss
21. Disease research org.
24. Chemical used to fight malaria
25. Brazilian city
26. Nevertheless
28. Quick swim
30. Phone bk. info
31. Test for PhD wannabes
32. Bill Clinton's instrument
34. Graduating class

36. Mummifies

39. *The Real World* network

41. Command to a dog

44. "It follows that…"

46. Rationed, with "out"

47. ___'acte (intermission)

48. Classic soft drink

49. Rhythm instrument

51. Nod off

52. Laura of *Jurassic Park*

53. Move in the breeze

56. Sing without words

Solution on Page 274

ACROSS

1. Henpecks
5. Cal.'s ocean
8. Stiffly neat
12. "___ Wanna Do" (Sheryl Crow tune)
13. Airport monitor abbr.
14. ___ Strauss jeans
15. Digital music player
16. ___ tee (exactly)
17. Switchboard worker: abbr.
18. Investment firm T. ___ Price
19. Primitive home
20. Amount of medicine to take
21. Droopy-eared hounds
24. Less cooked
27. Elizabethan or Victorian
28. Hosp. test
31. Privileged few
32. Dark ale
34. Foil metal
35. Alternative to "Woof!"
38. Latin dance
39. Tipped off
41. Amazes
44. Co. bigwig
45. ___ Alto, Calif.
49. "Do I have to draw you ___?"
50. "All you had to do was ___"
51. "Your turn," to a walkie-talkie user
52. Marathon or sprint
53. SSW's reverse
54. Ding-a-___ (airhead)
55. 1982 Disney sci-fi film
56. Ship's weight unit
57. Whirling current

DOWN

1. Hair removal brand
2. Big name in dog food
3. Moonshine
4. Auxiliary wager
5. Routes
6. Stir up
7. Moon depression
8. Walks wearily
9. ___ *Man* (1984 Estevez film)
10. Currier's partner
11. Oozy ground
22. "It's been ___ pleasure"
23. Have a sample of
24. Part of AARP: abbr.
25. Thrilla in Manila fighter
26. "...___ one for the Gipper"
28. Calendar abbr.
29. Alternative to a bare floor
30. "Was ___ blame?"
33. Future frog
36. Take back, as testimony
37. City in California's Central Valley

144

39. Colorado resort
40. Subway coin
41. Toad feature
42. Sharif of *Lawrence of Arabia*
43. Site of the 1993 Branch Davidian siege
46. Like a superfan

47. Borrow's opposite
48. Wild time

Solution on Page 274

ACROSS

1. Newton fruit
4. Apple alternative
7. Rapper Snoop ___
11. Israeli firearm
12. Sudden wind
14. Caribbean liquors
15. Training run
16. Therefore
17. Shamu or Willy
18. Imbeciles
20. Gaza Strip grp.
22. Frontiersman Carson
23. Gave a hand
27. March 17 honoree, for short
30. Put on a blacklist
31. "Now I ___ me down to sleep…"
32. Gone
33. "___ Your Head on My Shoulder"
34. Broad bean
35. Buck Rogers player Gerard
36. One side of an issue
37. Sheets, pillowcases, etc.
38. Not more than
40. Stylish, in the '60s
41. Caesar's three
42. Lacking vitality
46. "Janie's Got ___" (Aerosmith song)
49. "It's either you ___"
51. High-tech "fingerprint"
52. Antiaircraft fire
53. "…___ the twain shall meet"
54. Natural tanner
55. Pulls along behind
56. Score components: abbr.
57. Prefix with center or dermis

DOWN

1. Japan's highest mountain
2. Polo Ralph Lauren competitor
3. "Thank Heaven for Little Girls" musical
4. Phrase of understanding
5. Explode
6. Chinese food additive
7. Emulate Pavlov's dogs
8. ___ *Town* (Thornton Wilder play)
9. Big inits. in trucks
10. Brownies' org.
13. Formal headgear
19. "Agreed!"
21. Football Hall of Famer Dawson
24. Lay out in advance
25. House overhang
26. Actress Cannon
27. Long, involved story
28. Twerp
29. Tree in Miami
30. Hot dog holder
33. Magical drink

34. Bona ___ (genuine)

36. ___: *Miami*

37. Recluses

39. Pig sounds

40. *Glengarry Glen Ross* playwright David

43. Store inventory: abbr.

44. ___ to one's neck

45. Child's plea

46. Toward the back of a ship

47. Day-___ paints

48. Big Detroit inits.

50. Member of the House, for short

Solution on Page 274

ACROSS

1. Singer La ___ Jackson
5. K–O filler
8. "Life is like ___ of chocolates"
12. Crazy-sounding bird
13. Nay canceler
14. Wedding reception centerpiece
15. Gulp down
16. Lung protector
17. *Moonstruck* actress
18. Plow animals
20. Fixes
21. Humpback, e.g.
24. Derek and Diddley
25. Suddenly bright stars
26. Tabloid fodder
29. It ended Nov. 11, 1918
30. Hanks film
31. *Invasion of the Body Snatchers* container
33. Gets around
36. Grating, as a voice
38. Going through
39. Win by ___
40. Label with a name on it
43. High-end German cars
45. Awful-smelling
46. Wine and dine, say
47. Genie's grant
51. "Pay ___ mind"
52. Camera choice, in brief
53. Prefix with lateral
54. Sound of discomfort
55. Took the gold
56. Invitation inits.

DOWN

1. Motherly ministering, for short
2. "Wow!"
3. "___ and Me Against the World"
4. Zambia neighbor
5. Ancient Greek instrument
6. Lo ___ (noodle dish)
7. Catch, as a crook
8. Gain entry to
9. German highway
10. Approved
11. Gen-___ (post-boom babies)
19. Illiterates' signatures
20. Cal. pages
21. U-turn from ESE
22. Hockey legend Gordie
23. Tel ___, Israel
24. Where cranberries grow
26. USO show audience
27. ___ facto
28. Bursts, as a balloon
30. Arthur of *The Golden Girls*
32. Color, as Easter eggs
34. Frankie of *Beach Blanket Bingo*

35. Understand, in hippie lingo

36. Like most sushi

37. "Is that your final ___?"

40. "Correct me ___ wrong…"

41. "What did I ___ deserve this?"

42. Bluefin or yellowfin

43. String tie

44. Poet's dawn

46. Opposite of ENE

48. Mensa members have high ones

49. Ford Explorer, e.g.

50. ___ flask (liquor container)

Solution on Page 275

ACROSS

1. British fliers: abbr.
4. Sets the dogs (on)
8. Custard base
11. Web auction site
13. Speak highly of
14. ___ soup (dense fog)
15. Aloe ___ (lotion ingredient)
16. Cat or engine sound
17. Restroom, for short
18. Informal language
20. Level of achievement
22. Cincinnati sitcom station
24. "___ out!" (ump's cry)
25. Professional no. cruncher
27. Ishmael's captain
30. Find attractive
33. Blubber
34. Nasal congestion locale
36. Dracula alter ego
37. Nightclub of song
39. Lovett of country music
40. Young ___
41. Ignited, as a match
43. Places for experiments
45. Like some cell phone charges
49. ___ Arabia
52. Merchandise ID
53. ___-back (relaxed)
55. In a ___ (teed off)
56. Nectar gatherer
57. DVR pioneer
58. Search
59. Football distances: abbr.
60. Large number
61. Sound heard in a herd

DOWN

1. Guns, as a motor
2. Brother of Cain and Seth
3. Exotic destinations
4. Motor oil additive
5. Cash substitutes
6. Rudely brief
7. Homeless animal
8. Phrase on the back of a buck
9. Camping stuff
10. "I ___ at the office"
12. Pull sharply
19. Mardi ___
21. Part of AT&T: abbr.
23. TV's Donahue
25. Roman 300
26. Former amateur
28. "Pick a number, ___ number"
29. China shop menace
31. Alternative to KS
32. Aliens, for short
35. Sail the seven ___
38. "Ready, ___, fire!"

150

42. Leans to one side

44. Big shindig

45. Red gem

46. Newspaper essay

47. It's on the tip of one's finger

48. Donate

50. Pet on *The Flintstones*

51. *Leave ___ Beaver*

54. ___ Jones Industrial

Solution on Page 275

ACROSS

1. *Play It ___, Sam*
6. Sound of a punch
9. Sunday talk: abbr.
12. Licorice-like flavoring
13. Mediterranean, for one
14. Yoko who loved John Lennon
15. Grass garment
17. Dentists' org.
18. "Give ___ little time"
19. Prerecorded
21. ___ Major (Big Dipper's constellation)
24. Thanksgiving, e.g.: abbr.
27. ___ d'oeuvres
28. Second-year students, for short
30. Songwriters' grp.
32. Overwhelming wonder
33. Jazz pianist Chick
35. Big elephant feature
38. "Hasta la vista!"
40. ___ Jean Baker (Marilyn Monroe)
42. Water barrier
44. Prof.'s degree
46. Risqué
47. A Hatfield, to a McCoy
49. "Don't mind ___ do"
51. When a plane is due in, for short
52. Deserted
58. Bride's new title
59. Letters after CD
60. Homer epic
61. Tofu source
62. Decimal point
63. Pennies

DOWN

1. Contented sigh
2. Bearded beast of Africa
3. Need a doctor's care
4. Old Testament prophet
5. Robin's home
6. Next-to-last Greek letter
7. "___ the ramparts we watched…"
8. Light bulb unit
9. Afternoon TV fare
10. Terminator
11. Highways and byways
16. Krazy ___
20. "Oh, I see!"
21. It's south of Can.
22. Use the oars
23. Roaring Twenties nightspot
25. Like Siberian winters
26. Put to a purpose
29. Phys. or chem.
31. Bottle alternative
34. Alley in the comics
36. Car co. bought by Chrysler
37. *The Illustrated Man* author Bradbury

39. Rep.'s rival

41. Baltimore baseballer

42. Judges to be

43. Foreword, for short

45. Loud commotion

48. Three feet

50. Bank acct. guarantor

53. Halloween cry

54. Quantity: abbr.

55. Diarist Anaïs

56. Do lunch, say

57. Letters after a cavity filler's name

Solution on Page 275

ACROSS

1. Wall St. opening
4. ___-à-porter (ready-to-wear)
8. Hair untangler
12. Potter pal Weasley
13. Regulation
14. Wonky
15. Classroom replacement
16. Certain computers
17. Big party
18. Work at a keyboard
20. ___ *Sun Also Rises*
22. Delivery org.
25. "___ your instructions…"
29. Vases
32. Tasting of wood, as some wines
34. Lucy of *Kill Bill*
35. Ft. or yd., e.g.
36. Educ. group
37. Frog's home
38. Verve
39. Notable achievement
40. Teensy
41. Underground Railroad "passenger"
43. Untouchable Eliot
45. "It's a mouse!"
47. RPM indicator
50. Metal thread
53. Flow like mud
56. Something to stand on
58. Whiz at tennis serves
59. Stick in one's ___ (rankle)
60. Provide with weapons
61. Seeks office
62. Places for holsters
63. Stew holder

DOWN

1. Form 1040 agcy.
2. Mope
3. "Walk ___" (Dionne Warwick hit)
4. Uses a lever
5. Abrade
6. Shade tree
7. Examination
8. Bistros
9. Have a debt
10. *The A-Team* star
11. "Catch ya later!"
19. "___ in Boots"
21. Manger contents
23. *The ___ of Greenwich Village* (1984 movie)
24. Prince of Darkness
26. Parcel of land
27. One, to Hans
28. Former mayor Giuliani
29. Baseball officials
30. Fishing line holder
31. Auto parts giant
33. *Kiss Me, ___*

PUZZLE 72

37. Leaning Tower's city

39. Agent's 15%, e.g.

42. Swerves

44. One-pot dinners

46. Former New York mayor Ed

48. Start an ovation

49. Rescuer, to a rescuee

50. Armed conflict

51. Hospital area with many IVs

52. Stimpy's TV pal

54. "Either you do it, ___ will!"

55. Nuke

57. Clock-setting std.

Solution on Page 275

ACROSS

1. Word with pick or wit
4. Software program, for short
7. Gorilla researcher Fossey
11. Consumed
12. Warty hopper
14. Online crafts marketplace
15. Opal or onyx
17. James of *The Godfather*
18. Popeye's Olive
19. Thin
21. Arkin and Alda
24. Weather-vane turner
25. Sloppy Joe holders
26. Drives recklessly
29. Birthday cake number
30. Confused fight
31. One, to Fritz
33. Leaves high and dry
35. Football's Crimson Tide, for short
36. Enthusiastic about
37. Condor's nest
38. Tennis champ Goolagong
41. "Dr." with Grammys
42. Hobby shop purchases
43. Brightness regulator
48. 1986 Nobel Peace Prize winner Wiesel
49. "I ___ to recall…"
50. Gorilla or gibbon
51. Small pouches
52. Rx watchdog
53. Train depot: abbr.

DOWN

1. Racehorse, slangily
2. Suffix with Israel
3. President pro ___
4. Lawyers: abbr.
5. Office wagering
6. ___-Hellenic (like the ancient Olympics)
7. Make up one's mind
8. "I'd consider ___ honor"
9. As strong ___ ox
10. Big Apple address letters
13. Longs for
16. Daughters' counterparts
20. Elbow's lower counterpart
21. Legal org.
22. Drags along
23. Work without ___
24. Ralph ___ Emerson
26. Midpoints
27. Not far away
28. ___ Valley (Reagan Library city)
30. *The Magic Mountain* author
32. Scottish denial
34. Gets the soap off
35. Nectar collectors

37. Nasal stimulus

38. Squeezes (out)

39. '80s *This Old House* host Bob

40. Auricular

41. Proof of title

44. *Playboy* founder, familiarly

45. Prof's helpers

46. Prone

47. Gymnast's perfect score

Solution on Page 276

ACROSS

1. Ranting and raving
4. Butter square
7. Edinburgh native
11. "I've Got ___ in Kalamazoo"
13. AP competitor
14. Get by somehow
15. Agatha Christie's *And Then There Were ___*
16. Headstone letters
17. Lot of land
18. Ream unit
20. Baseball great Willie
21. ___ nova (Brazilian dance)
24. Mechanical teeth
26. Great Lakes Indians
27. Squiggly swimmer
28. Sporty Pontiac
31. Actress Moorehead
32. Standoffish
34. "For shame!"
35. ___ Tzu (Taoism founder)
38. Draws nigh
39. Repressed, with "up"
40. West Pointer
41. ___ San Lucas, Mexico
44. Carries
46. Poems of praise
47. Word with down or key
48. Thompson of *Sense and Sensibility*
52. Totally uncool
53. Gin maker Whitney
54. Hand out cards
55. Yes votes
56. ___ US Pat. Off.
57. Small batteries

DOWN

1. To a ___ (without exception)
2. Many moons ___
3. Blues Brother Aykroyd
4. Untainted
5. For each
6. Walk softly
7. Con jobs
8. ___-Cola
9. Grand Ole ___
10. Caddie's pocketful
12. Tenant
19. Give a hard time
21. Outscore
22. Societies: abbr.
23. Go under
25. Brief look
28. Egg on
29. Shredded
30. *Spirit ___ Louis*
33. Rented
36. Horn
37. *Lawrence of Arabia* star

39. Sits for a portrait

41. Fast-food drink

42. "An apple ___…"

43. Sammy Davis Jr.'s "I've Gotta ___"

45. Tiny branch

49. "Tell ___ story"

50. Calf call

51. Pacino and Capone

Solution on Page 276

ACROSS

1. Web conversation
5. Tight hold
9. Dictator Amin
12. "___ goes nothing!"
13. Costa ___
14. Actress Ullmann
15. Durante's "___ Dinka Doo"
16. Green gems
18. NNE's opposite
20. Drive headlong into
21. Like Georgia Brown
24. Color changers
28. Tariff
29. Loosen, as a knot
33. M–Q link
34. Many a time
35. Put money (on)
36. Datebook abbr.
37. Occupational suffix
38. Rice field
40. And others, for short
41. Wrecking-ball swinger
43. Units of farmland
45. Klutzy sort
47. Weed-whacking tool
48. Move to another country
52. Walk with a hitch
56. Attack command to Fido
57. Author O'Flaherty
58. Hardly ___ (rarely)
59. Take care of a bill
60. Woman's undergarment
61. Computer memory measure

DOWN

1. Letter before psi
2. Coop brooder
3. Flood floater
4. Flirty one
5. Sprouted
6. Edge of a hoop
7. Cake finisher
8. Memorial Day event
9. "___ have what she's having" (line from *When Harry Met Sally…*)
10. "The butler ___ it"
11. ICU drips
17. Singer Grant
19. R–V connection
21. Stiff-upper-lip type
22. Thin cookie
23. Movie crowd member
25. Step inside
26. MapQuest offering
27. Eyeglasses, for short
30. Lakers' org.
31. Kennedy or Koppel
32. "___ be an honor"
38. Bits of wisdom?

39. Basketball's ___ Ming

42. Yuletide beverage

44. Star

46. Flunk

47. Rope fiber

48. Paranormal power, for short

49. ABBA's "Mamma ___"

50. Slippery, as winter sidewalks

51. ___ chi (Chinese discipline)

53. Wall climber

54. Bumped into

55. ___-Columbian era

Solution on Page 276

ACROSS

1. ___ and Span (cleaner brand)
5. Law degs.
8. Karate blow
12. "Round and Round" singer Perry
13. Operated
14. Des Moines's state
15. Meter or liter
16. Reagan's Star Wars prog.
17. *Ain't Misbehavin'* star Carter
18. Fender flaws
20. Shells out
22. Mil. mail drop
24. Braun or Perón
25. Falls on the border
29. Online letter
33. Wile E. Coyote's supply company
34. Concorde, e.g.
36. Ye ___ Curiosity Shoppe
37. Show the ropes to
39. Unhappy state
41. Right off the stove
43. ___'easter
44. Looked lecherously
47. Forbidden acts
51. ___ one's time (wait)
52. Hi-___ monitor
54. Barn area where hay is kept
55. Submachine guns
56. Yale School of Drama deg.
57. Debussy's "Clair de ___"
58. Life partner
59. Pig's home
60. Skier's wish

DOWN

1. Gulf War missile
2. Johnnycake
3. Porter's "___ Love Again"
4. Dairy case item
5. Third-year students: abbr.
6. Fathers
7. Make nasty comments
8. Sticky breakfast sweets
9. Broke some ground
10. Wise birds
11. Bert, to Ernie
19. Spot for a seaweed wrap
21. Adam's mate
23. Surgery sites, for short
25. Enslaved Turner
26. Rocks, to a bartender
27. Org. with a noted journal
28. Donkey's cousin
30. India pale ___
31. Check-cashing needs
32. ___ *Misérables*
35. Bronze
38. Not vert.
40. ___ Juan (lover)

162

42. Contract provisions

44. Entertainer Minnelli

45. Fix text

46. Adept

48. Part of speech

49. ___ consequence (insignificant)

50. Meat and vegetables dish

51. Mooch, as a cigarette

53. "Needless to ___..."

Solution on Page 276

ACROSS

1. Spanish greeting
5. "___ ain't broke…"
9. Not quite oneself
12. Jump in an ice rink
13. Cartoonist Goldberg
14. Part of TGIF: abbr.
15. Winter coat material
16. Like an eagle's vision
17. Trail the pack
18. Fictional work
20. They may be reserved
22. Walking on air
24. Implore
25. Samuel with a code
26. Act like a sponge
29. Tiny amount
30. What a DJ speaks into
31. Continent north of Afr.
33. "Pretty good!"
36. Practical joke
38. *The ___ of the Jackal*
39. Takes care of
40. *___ from the Past*
43. Does damage to
44. Slice (off)
45. State north of Calif.
47. On the ___ (not speaking)
50. One: prefix
51. Branching-out point
52. Ensnare
53. Jury-___ (improvise)
54. Beans used for tofu
55. Hair-raising

DOWN

1. Partner of hem
2. Tic-tac-toe loser
3. Actor DiCaprio
4. Divvies up
5. Bothered
6. Energy source for engines
7. "May ___ frank?"
8. Past, present, and future
9. *Man ___ Mancha*
10. Toga party site
11. Mediterranean fruit trees
19. Peace sign shape
21. Swellhead's problem
22. CPR administrant
23. Credit union offering
24. Telly network
26. Assist
27. Restore confidence to
28. Short hit, in baseball
30. Mom's month
32. *It's a Wonderful Life* studio
34. QB's scores
35. Conductors' sticks
36. ___ diem

164

37. Distant

39. Wise ones

40. Become hazy

41. Actress Anderson

42. Eat like ___ (stuff oneself)

43. Actress Lamarr

46. Australian hopper, for short

48. Part of cigarette smoke

49. James Bond, for one

Solution on Page 277

ACROSS

1. Standard Windows typeface
6. Orbital path
9. "Open 9 ___ 6"
12. *The Count of ___ Cristo*
13. ___ Paulo
14. *Wheel of Fortune* buy
15. Arctic barkers
16. Small drink
17. Larry King's channel
18. Place for a lawn mower
20. Head honcho
21. Little troublemaker
24. Al of Indy
26. Fannie ___
27. Police dept. rank
28. Group of plotters
32. Handsome lad of myth
34. Spud
35. Voice above baritone
36. ___ mot (witticism)
37. Pan Am rival
38. Fall flower
40. Grass bought in rolls
41. Apt. part, in ads
44. Inauguration Day recital
46. ___ Claire, Wis.
47. Opposite of syn.
48. "Am not!" reply
53. Asner and Bradley
54. Luau neckwear
55. Throat ailment
56. ___ Tuesday (Mardi Gras)
57. Painting or sculpture
58. Exterminator's targets

DOWN

1. Grand ___ (sporty Pontiacs)
2. Sushi eggs
3. "All ___ day's work"
4. The "A" in NATO: abbr.
5. Amount to make do with
6. Concurrence
7. Fridge forays
8. Radar gun aimer
9. Mexican snack
10. Overnight lodgings
11. Eyeglass part
19. Holds close
20. Enfant terrible
21. "___ your disposal"
22. Constructed
23. Unappreciated worker
25. Subj. for Milton Friedman
27. Knights' titles
29. Belfry residents
30. "A-one and ___": Welk
31. Washing machine unit
33. Author Chomsky
34. Starboard's opposite

The following is a grid with numbers:

1	2	3	4	5		6	7	8		9	10	11
12						13				14		
15						16				17		
				18	19				20			
21	22	23			24			25				
26				27				28		29	30	31
32			33				34					
35					36				37			
			38		39				40			
41	42	43			44		45					
46				47				48	49	50	51	52
53				54				55				
56				57				58				

36. "Scram!"

39. Copier need

41. Hamburger meat

42. Early baby word

43. What stainless steel doesn't do

45. Hinged fastener

47. ___ mode (served with ice cream)

49. Road sign abbr.

50. Hosp. trauma centers

51. Two of a kind

52. Co-___ (condo relatives)

Solution on Page 277

ACROSS

1. Runs smoothly
5. *60 Minutes* airer
8. Tree branch
12. "It should come ___ surprise"
13. ___-been (faded star)
14. R.E.M.'s "The ___ Love"
15. Hired thug
16. Feeling of rage
17. Unconscious state
18. Just ___ (small amount, as of hair gel)
20. Peels
21. Dropped a line
24. Devil's doing
26. Title colonel in a 1960s sitcom
27. Hook-shaped New England peninsula
31. Night school subj.
32. Boy king of Egypt
33. Poem of praise
34. Blight on the landscape
37. One of the Osmonds
39. Consequently
40. ___ and wiser
41. PC storage medium
44. ___ mater
46. ___ Mountains (edge of Asia)
47. Imbiber's offense, briefly
48. Sober-motoring org.
52. Window part
53. Highest card
54. Merle Haggard's "___ From Muskogee"
55. Comical Laurel
56. "All ___ are created equal"
57. ___ Club (discount chain)

DOWN

1. Witch
2. Grp. putting on shows for troops
3. L–P filler
4. Beethoven's "Moonlight ___"
5. ___ Pet
6. It sticks to your ribs
7. Dir. opposite NNW
8. Place
9. "___ out?" (pet's choice)
10. Viral video, e.g.
11. Media slant
19. Comfy room
20. Playing card dot
21. Amusement park shout
22. Flushed, as cheeks
23. Give a longing look
25. Brewery container
28. Parachute part
29. Dog tormented by Garfield
30. ___ Xing (sign)
32. Capote, for short

35. Like some kisses and bases
36. Resistance unit that sounds like a meditation word
37. Popular tattoo
38. Los ___, NM
41. Parts of a tea set
42. "Doggone it!"

43. ___ fever (was sick)
45. Property claim
47. Flood control structure
49. Letters preceding an alias
50. Lower, as the lights
51. ___ *Moines Register*

Solution on Page 277

ACROSS

1. Scott of *Charles in Charge*
5. Jr. high, e.g.
8. Backyard cookouts, for short
12. "___ your side"
13. ___ and cry
14. Cause a stench
15. "___ lay me down…"
16. ___ Lingus (Irish airline)
17. Memorial Day weekend race, to fans
18. Artist's rendering
20. Eighth mo.
22. Biblical hymn
24. Ring decision, briefly
27. Do-nothing
31. Man from Boise
33. Relax in the tub
34. AARP members
35. Mixed-breed dog
36. Actress Bening
38. Midsection
39. Cultural funding grp.
40. The "R" of NPR
42. Insult, slangily
43. Androids
48. Small flute
51. SHO alternative
53. Vegetable in Cajun cuisine
54. Eye-color area
55. Suffix with north or south
56. Huffed and puffed
57. Combat vehicle
58. "Help!" signal
59. "Survey ___…" (*Family Feud* phrase)

DOWN

1. Storage containers
2. Totally out of control
3. "How much do ___ you?"
4. "Step ___!" ("Hurry up!")
5. Former Iranian leaders
6. Pool player's stick
7. Announces with fanfare
8. Naval lockup
9. Actor Affleck
10. Letters after a proof
11. Wild blue yonder
19. Lifesaving skill, for short
21. Thurman of Kill Bill films
23. Broadcast
24. ___ de France
25. Kit ___ (candy bars)
26. Catch ___ (start to get)
27. "No man ___ island"
28. Completed
29. Glamorous actress Turner
30. Scrape (by)
32. Medical insurance abbr.

34. Squirrels away

37. Prefix with angle or cycle

38. "Tippecanoe and Tyler ___"

41. Oscar winner Jeremy

42. Office necessity

44. Short hairdos

45. Tex. neighbor

46. Three, in cards

47. Lumberjack's tools

48. ___ to be tied (angry)

49. Nest egg abbr.

50. Fish propeller

52. Male buddy

Solution on Page 277

ACROSS

1. Actress ___ Dawn Chong
4. Baby elephant
8. Grease job
12. Often-hectic hosp. areas
13. One with debts
14. "___ to differ"
15. Insult, in slang
16. Advertising award
17. Tennis champ Björn
18. Former Roxy Music member Brian
20. Group spirit
22. Lunatic
25. Put on a scale of 1 to 10
26. 2.54 centimeters
27. "___ is not to reason why"
30. Philosopher Lao ___
31. Suffix with Siam
32. Alternatives to Macs
35. B–G connection
36. Red planet
37. Go on a buying spree
41. Gets underway
43. Give a hard time
45. Extra-wide, at the shoe store
46. Part of a list
47. "Am ___ only one?"
50. Govt. code breakers
53. Sukiyaki side dish
54. Not fat
55. Camel's color
56. Small children
57. Young fellows
58. Hog hangout

DOWN

1. Danger color
2. Former Bush press secretary Fleischer
3. Perfume
4. Drink served with marshmallows
5. Leatherworker's puncher
6. Hawaiian neckwear
7. ___ *Here to Eternity*
8. The Scales, astrologically
9. WWII vessel
10. TV's Uncle Miltie
11. Urged (on)
19. Fed. biomedical research agcy.
21. Hospital areas: abbr.
22. Cambridge univ.
23. The "A" of Q&A: abbr.
24. Like some dorms
28. In ___ (occupied)
29. Whistle blowers
32. Mom and pop
33. Old PC monitor type
34. Snaky sound
35. Bank offerings, briefly
36. Al Capp's Daisy ___

```
 1   2   3  ███  4   5   6   7  ███  8   9  10  11
12          ███ 13          ███ 14
15          ███ 16          ███ 17
███ 18  19          ███ 20  21
22  23          24      ███ 25
26          ███ 27  28  29      ███
30          ███ 31          ███ 32  33  34
███     35          ███     36
37  38  39  40      ███ 41  42
43          ███ 44      ███ 45      ███
46          ███ 47  48  49      ███ 50  51  52
53          ███ 54          ███ 55
56          ███ 57          ███ 58
```

37. Collared garment

38. Place for a cookout

39. Standing straight

40. Tom, Dick, and Harry, e.g.

42. Adolescents

44. Window base

48. Lipton offering

49. "I've ___ it up to here!"

51. Plunked oneself down

52. "___ takers?"

Solution on Page 278

ACROSS

1. Emulate Picabo Street
4. Rockies, e.g.
7. Ann ___, Mich.
12. Little ___ (tots)
13. King in a Steve Martin song
14. Rueful
15. Address book no.
16. Flying geese formation
17. Big
18. Atoll protector
20. Use a book
22. Take ___ at (try)
24. Bert Bobbsey's twin sister
25. The L of L.A.
28. Lowest quality
30. Co. photo badges, e.g.
31. Kind of cake
34. Hold back
37. Visible part of an iceberg
38. Backyard barrier
40. Brown truck co.
41. Race, as an engine
42. Epsom ___
46. Clinton's #2
47. Green fruit
48. "Have I got ___ for you!"
51. Opposite of SSE
54. Periodical, for short
55. Largest Greek island
56. Road surfacing material
57. "Ich ___ ein Berliner"
58. Little kids
59. Le Carré character
60. Add-___ (extras)

DOWN

1. Kama ___
2. Prayers are often said on them
3. Speck in the sea
4. Network with annual awards
5. Wed. preceder
6. Backs of boats
7. The Chronicles of Narnia lion
8. Highway
9. Shiverer's sound
10. www.aspca.___
11. Bread with caraway seeds
19. Young Bambi
21. Dine at home
23. Cranberry-growing site
25. "Let sleeping dogs ___"
26. Hardly ordinary
27. 180 from NNW
29. Allude (to)
31. VW predecessors?
32. *Great Expectations* boy
33. Photo ___ (publicity events)
35. Roast hosts, briefly
36. Summit

39. Occasions
41. Parts to play
43. State of uncertainty
44. *The Adventures of Tom Sawyer* author
45. Omens
46. California's Golden ___ Bridge

48. Perform on a stage
49. Arid
50. Mouse hater's cry
52. Quick snooze
53. Dryly humorous

Solution on Page 278

ACROSS

1. Figs.
4. Light knock
7. Undulating
11. Pen filler
12. ___-K (before kindergarten)
13. Nephew of Donald Duck
14. Sheep's call
15. It might say WELCOME
16. "Like a Rock" singer Bob
17. Create a lap
18. Rosary unit
20. Third man in the ring
22. Theory suffix
23. Remind too often
26. Sony rival
28. Jewish mystical doctrine
31. Olympic sleds
34. Highway exits
35. Titillating
37. Frequently
38. ___-Cat (winter vehicle)
39. Photo, for short
41. "Every dog ___ its day"
44. Speedy
45. Windows predecessor
47. Listerine alternative
51. Captain's record on *Star Trek*
53. Expected
54. Expressed wonder
55. iPhone download
56. Trojans' sch.
57. "___ and Circumstance"
58. Prefix with place or print
59. Salary

DOWN

1. Writing points
2. Broadcast studio sign
3. Glide on the ice
4. Meas. of engine speed
5. Saudi ___
6. "For ___ sake!"
7. Hardship
8. Jul. follower
9. Compete
10. "___ darn tootin'!"
13. '60s hallucinogenic
19. *Mad Men* cable channel
21. Ridge on a guitar neck
23. *Apocalypse Now* setting, briefly
24. Mont Blanc, e.g.
25. Heating fuel
27. CBS forensic drama
29. Dog's bark
30. Soaking site
31. ___ Paul guitars
32. Large coffee vessel
33. Gunk
36. Tax form expert: abbr.

PUZZLE 83

37. Eight-armed creatures
40. Religion of the Koran
42. Find the sum of
43. Composer of marches
44. Prime rate setter, with “the”
46. Cabinet member: abbr.
47. Absorb, with “up”
48. Dovish sound
49. Bit of resistance
50. Zest
52. Modern navigation syst.

Solution on Page 278

ACROSS

1. Canine warning
4. "___ be darned!"
7. Keats, for one
11. Seek the affections of
12. Pup's bites
14. Not prerecorded
15. Superlative ending
16. Not fem.
17. Haley who wrote *Roots*
18. Drink of the gods
20. Competed in a 10K
22. UFO crew
23. Franklin known as the Queen of Soul
27. Number of Little Pigs
30. Tax-filing mo.
31. She, objectively
32. Kitchen or den
33. "Tiptoe Thru' the Tulips with Me" instrument
34. Cir. bisector
35. "___ Yankee Doodle Dandy"
36. Genetic carrier
37. Macho
38. Tasty tidbit
40. Berlin's country: abbr.
41. Also
42. Restaurant activity
46. Michelle, to Barack
49. Street ___ (reputation)
51. Parental palindrome
52. Whirled
53. Vegas numbers game
54. Boise's state: abbr.
55. "This ___ take long"
56. Crow's cry
57. In a merry mood

DOWN

1. Singer Stefani
2. Valentine's Day flower
3. Campus mil. program
4. Prisoner
5. Fibbers
6. Record collector's platters
7. 747, e.g.
8. Crankcase fluid
9. 12/31, e.g.
10. Country singer Ritter
13. Abrasion
19. Be abundant (with)
21. Airport abbr.
24. Significantly underweight
25. Cure
26. Fighting force
27. Adjust, as sails
28. ___ erectus
29. Lion's warning
30. Abbr. before an alias

33. Open with a key
34. Pub projectile
36. Speed Wagon maker
37. Pasture
39. Cardiologist's insert
40. Davis of *A League of Their Own*
43. "Gotcha"

44. Nothing, in Spain
45. Aussie's greeting
46. U-turn from ENE
47. Nasdaq debut: abbr.
48. Amusement
50. Amusement, for short

Solution on Page 278

ACROSS

1. Two-___ paper towels
4. Poker variety
8. Lubricates
12. Hugs, symbolically
13. Sound of surprise
14. Service charges
15. University URL ending
16. Bridle strap
17. QB Tarkenton
18. Parisian thanks
20. ___ Bo (exercise system)
22. Cheryl of *Charlie's Angels*
25. Pokes
29. Havana's home
32. New Haven university
34. "___ on Goodness" (*Camelot* song)
35. Hideous
36. Big bird Down Under
37. Martian invasion report, e.g.
38. However, briefly
39. La ___ Tar Pits
40. Osbourne of Black Sabbath
41. Cosmetics maker Lauder
43. Totals
45. Data-sharing syst.
47. Garden insect
51. Pole or Czech
54. Part of a nuclear arsenal, for short
57. "___ making myself clear?"
58. Golfer's target
59. Fraction of a kilo
60. Scot's refusal
61. Red ___ (cinnamon candies)
62. Georgetown athlete
63. Sock hop locale

DOWN

1. Wordsworth work
2. Rich vein
3. Part of BYOB
4. Where Damascus is capital
5. Item with a clip or a pin
6. News org. created in 1958
7. Bumper blemish
8. Auction bid
9. Suffix with cash, cloth, or hotel
10. Grassy field
11. Payroll ID
19. Sculptor's medium
21. Animal that beats its chest
23. Hair colorer
24. Knights' wives
26. *The Wizard* ___
27. Actress Cameron
28. "I'm too ___ for my shirt" (Right Said Fred lyric)
29. ___ as a button
30. Sounds of displeasure
31. Ink stain
33. Hawaiian shindig

37. Med. center
39. Arthur of *Maude*
42. Santa's helpers
44. "___ mia!"
46. Close by, in poetry
48. Get the ___ of (learn)
49. "___ be wrong, but…"

50. Carpe ___
51. "Quiet, please!"
52. Lavatory, in London
53. Ctrl-___-Delete
55. Magnon start
56. San Francisco/Oakland separator

Solution on Page 279

ACROSS

1. King with a golden touch
6. *Sesame Street* broadcaster
9. Bilko or Friday: abbr.
12. Oil company that merged with BP
13. Sam ___ (Dr. Seuss character)
14. Crib cry
15. Relating to bees
16. U-turn from SSW
17. "How can ___ sure?"
18. Steals, with "off"
20. ___-craftsy
22. Attractiveness
25. Capote, on Broadway
26. 66, e.g.: abbr.
27. Degrades
30. Painter Chagall
32. Ship's call for help
33. Sunrise
36. Clarence of the Supreme Court
38. DiCaprio, to pals
39. Pigs ___ blanket
40. Egg hunt holiday
43. Box for oranges
46. Radar sign
47. Alley ___
48. Post-op area
50. Paper quantities
54. Suffix for suburban
55. On, as a lamp
56. Follow
57. *The X-Files* network
58. It's perpendicular to long.
59. Post office purchase

DOWN

1. Lamb's cry
2. Little devil
3. "___ have to?"
4. Without ___ in the world
5. Actress Braga
6. Bowlers' targets
7. Test-___ treaty
8. Applies, as finger paint
9. Houlihan portrayer
10. Chews the fat
11. "___ went thataway!"
19. Liquid part of blood
21. Was sorry about
22. Quarterback's asset
23. School grp.
24. Bouncy
25. Graduation cap attachment
28. Feathery wrap
29. Pretzel covering
31. Gambler's marker
34. Itsy-bitsy
35. Neither fish ___ fowl
37. *The Iceman Cometh* playwright Eugene

41. Buenos ___, Argentina

42. Laid out, as cash

43. Hairdo

44. Prefix with tiller

45. Very top

46. Ashtray item

49. Spy org.

51. Flat ___ pancake

52. Britain's Queen ___

53. Autumn mo.

Solution on Page 279

ACROSS

1. Mo. metropolis
4. Condescending type
8. MGM symbol
12. KFC's Sanders, e.g.
13. Chanel of fashion
14. Cats' prey
15. "Now ___ theater near you!"
16. Disguised
18. Do–fa connection
20. Beyond doubt
21. Lou Grant portrayer
23. Road rollers
28. Novelist Deighton
29. At peace
30. Brews, as tea
33. Change over time
34. Despise
35. Signer's need
36. Find a new purpose for
37. Lynn Redgrave's sister
41. Fan sound
43. Specks
44. Revolving tray
49. In good physical shape
50. Decked out (in)
51. Say ___ (turn down)
52. "I'll take that as ___"
53. Excavates
54. Diver Louganis
55. Train stop: abbr.

DOWN

1. Terrify
2. Lugged along
3. Peruvian beast
4. Poli ___ (college major)
5. Baloney
6. Come to pass
7. Unmannered fellow
8. Trio before O
9. 3:00, on a sundial
10. Sept. follower
11. Keanu in *The Matrix*
17. Settle a score
19. Archipelago parts
22. Huey, Dewey, and Louie, to Donald
24. Pressed, as clothes
25. Aunt or uncle: abbr.
26. Part of SASE
27. "Monkey ___, monkey do"
29. Divide
30. Popular camera type, for short
31. Stubbed digit
32. ___ de cologne
37. Eyeshade
38. Couches

39. Tour of duty

40. ___ Martin (James Bond car)

42. Deadlocked, as a jury

44. Calc. display

45. Boxer Muhammad

46. Zig's partner

47. Units of three feet: abbr.

48. Eggy beverage

Solution on Page 279

ACROSS

1. Airwaves regulatory grp.
4. It's north of Mex.
7. ___ Raton, Fla.
11. Singer Rawls or Reed
12. Phoenix hoopsters
14. Wetlands plant
15. Find a sum
16. Warmth
17. Internet addresses
18. Tried out
20. Go to seed
22. "___ you kidding me?"
23. Puts forth, as effort
27. Stinks
30. ___ Paulo, Brazil
31. Thumbs-up
32. Massages
33. Tree in many street names
34. Tom's ex before Nicole
35. 1950s prez
36. "Our ___ Will Come"
37. Oregon capital
38. Yellowstone attraction
40. It may have 2 BRs
41. Make lace
42. Daytona 500 org.
46. ___ B'rith
49. "___ it going?"
51. "Now I've got it!"
52. Gooey cheese
53. In ___ (stuck)
54. Poker prize
55. Rotating engine parts
56. Upper class: abbr.
57. TV's Science Guy

DOWN

1. Off key
2. Morse ___
3. Cows chew them
4. Wedding helpers
5. Napped leather
6. ___ for effort
7. Big bully
8. "___ the fields we go…"
9. Cartoon frame
10. Internet popups
13. Creek
19. Paves
21. Nonwinning tic-tac-toe line
24. Stairway safety feature
25. Heavy volume
26. Glance through quickly
27. Not a dup.
28. Home of the Blue Devils
29. Do as one's told
30. Clever like a fox
33. Singer Kitt
34. Wrestling surfaces

36. Narc's org.

37. Muscle twitches

39. Pigpens

40. Sadat of Egypt

43. ___ Crunch (Quaker cereal)

44. Chips ___! (cookie brand)

45. Hourly charge

46. Network on the telly

47. Gun grp.

48. "We ___ to please!"

50. Some IHOP drinks

Solution on Page 279

ACROSS

1. Bygone airline
4. Slumber party garb
7. I, in Innsbruck?
10. Aluminum wrap
11. Org. that gets members reduced motel rates
12. Disparaging remark
14. Font property, sometimes
15. Heavens
16. ___-tat (snare drum sound)
17. Passionate
19. ___ and raves
20. Like steak tartare
21. Actress Jamie ___ Curtis
22. Cash dispenser, briefly
25. 1990 Macaulay Culkin film
30. *Voyager* launcher
32. Critic Reed
33. "___ pronounce you…"
34. Simple swimming stroke
37. Suffix with lemon or lime
38. Tony Blair and others, briefly
39. Geller with a psychic act
41. Leers at
44. ___ of limitations
48. Dog biter
49. ___ and aah
50. Potato, informally
51. Obscures, with "up"
52. Batman and Robin are a "dynamic" one
53. Unruly crowds
54. Broadway's *Five Guys Named* ___
55. Mess up
56. 180 from WSW

DOWN

1. Roger Rabbit, e.g.
2. Droop, as flowers
3. Tree of the birch family
4. Computer access codes
5. Boxer LaMotta
6. Vocalize
7. Tel Aviv native
8. *The ___ of the Cave Bear*
9. Jabba the ___ of Star Wars films
10. J. Edgar Hoover's grp.
13. Univ. dorm supervisors
18. "Nope"
19. *The Crying Game* star Stephen
21. "Superman" villain
22. Ampersand
23. Lao Tzu's *Tao Te Ching*
24. No ___ (Chinese menu notation)
26. ___ school
27. Bon Jovi's "Livin' ___ Prayer"
28. Doze (off)
29. Lamb's mama
31. Mollify

35. Morning hrs.

36. Mesozoic or Paleozoic

40. Reply to "Who's there?"

41. Not at work

42. ___ onto (grab)

43. Toy block brand

44. Whiskey drink

45. "___ the Roof" (Drifters hit)

46. TV, slangily, with "the"

47. Koch and Asner

49. Beethoven's "___ to Joy"

Solution on Page 280

ACROSS

1. Body of salt water
4. One way to get directions
7. Lip-___ (not really sing)
11. Quaint lodging
12. Tai ___ (exercise method)
13. Italian goodbye
14. Announcer Pardo
15. Course after trig
17. Gem with colored bands
18. Escape detection of
20. Free of clutter
22. Dish of greens
23. Clothing
27. State of rest
30. Little lie
31. "What the ___!"
34. Bar beverage
35. Bee Gees family name
36. Somewhat: suffix
37. Magician's word
39. Heavy hammer
41. Bridle straps
45. Magician's stick
47. Golfer Palmer, familiarly
48. Zoo unit
51. Sea swallow
53. Former AT&T rival
54. Munch
55. Lobbying grp.
56. Run-of-the-mill: abbr.
57. Neatnik's opposite
58. "___ end"
59. ___ with (tease)

DOWN

1. Slaw, fries, etc.
2. WWII plane ___ Gay
3. Invalidate
4. Agree (to)
5. Al Green's "___-La-La"
6. Ceramist's oven
7. F. ___ Fitzgerald
8. Yang's complement
9. Dissenting vote
10. Courteney of Friends
16. Puts an end to
19. Like the night
21. Had supper
24. "___ Were King"
25. What Eve was formed from
26. Tidal retreat
28. Mother or father
29. Spanish cheer
31. ___ and hers
32. Immigrant's subj.
33. Señor Guevara
35. Ending for "theater" or "church"
37. Mickelson's org.
38. Hypnotic state

40. Nerd

42. Gold bar

43. Part of TNT

44. Run-down in appearance, as a motel

46. Part of USDA: abbr.

48. *Survivor* network

49. Feel unwell

50. Powerful Pontiac

52. Short cheer

Solution on Page 280

ACROSS

1. Graffiti signature
4. Home loan agcy.
7. Workers on duty
12. *King Kong* studio
13. Online chuckle
14. Worshiper of Brahma
15. Financial support
16. Barn bird
17. Writer ___ Allan Poe
18. Ont. or Que.
20. Lazily
22. Sleek fabric
24. Slithery fish
25. Have an evening meal
28. Seashore
30. Speakers' hesitations
31. Put a match to
34. Agree to
37. The Sunshine St.
38. "Life ___ short…"
40. Boo-hoo
41. Holy Trinity member
42. "God ___ America"
46. Passage for Santa
47. Word book: abbr.
48. Physics Nobelist Marie
51. Wapiti
54. Test for coll. seniors
55. Atmospheric layer
56. Mark of Zorro
57. Farm fowl
58. Dalai Lama's land
59. ___ drop soup
60. What it takes to tango

DOWN

1. Snares
2. Director Kurosawa
3. Beckett's *Waiting for* ___
4. Waitress at Mel's Diner
5. "___ do you do?"
6. Axis foes
7. Turtle's covering
8. Neat
9. Taiwanese-born director Lee
10. Pharmaceuticals watchdog agcy.
11. PETA peeve
19. "Veni, vidi, ___"
21. Coup ___
23. Part of NIMBY
25. Haul into court
26. "Steee-rike!" caller
27. L.A. clock setting
29. Vowel sequence
31. Contingencies
32. Mop & ___: cleaning brand
33. Catch in the act
35. Kernel holder
36. Not hot

PUZZLE 91

39. Reason to say "Gesundheit!"

41. Icy precipitation

43. Two cubed

44. Threaded fastener

45. Court reporter

46. Speeder's penalty

48. Barracks bunk

49. Israeli gun

50. Steal

52. Turkey portion

53. Beer container

Solution on Page 280

ACROSS

1. When doubled, a dance
4. ___-la-la
7. RKO competitor
10. Doofus
11. It's all around you
12. Faulkner's As ___ Dying
14. Tug-of-war equipment
15. Atlanta-based public health agcy.
16. Bait and switch, e.g.
17. On the line
19. Light bulb units
20. Fa follower
21. Hawaiian Punch alternative
22. Air conditioner meas.
25. They protect car buyers
30. Colt's mother
32. London's Big ___
33. Basic util.
34. Self-control
37. Bit of fireplace residue
38. Calif. airport
39. "Are we having fun ___?"
41. Blacksmith's block
44. Current units
48. Spike and Bruce
49. Game of Thrones channel
50. Long, angry complaint
51. ___-Japanese War
52. Kanga's kid
53. Soapy froth
54. Palindromic diarist
55. Wd. in Roget's
56. "Don't Bring Me Down" band, for short

DOWN

1. Geezer
2. Bunny movements
3. Helps with a heist
4. Fishing gear holder
5. Merry-go-round or roller coaster
6. Path of a fly ball
7. ___ on 34th Street
8. Excess supply
9. Boom support
10. Lingerie purchase
13. "Agreed"
18. "You've got mail" co.
19. Triumph
21. Newlyweds' trip
22. Autobahn auto
23. Mai ___ (bar order)
24. Internet address, briefly
26. Kitten's cry
27. ___ carte (menu phrase)
28. Scream director Craven
29. PTA mtg. place
31. Ralph who wrote Invisible Man
35. "Be a ___!"

36. Sales agent, for short

40. Far from wordy

41. Jolson and Jarreau

42. No, in Nuremberg

43. "___, vidi, vici" (Caesar's boast)

44. Johnny Cash's "___ Named Sue"

45. Julia of *The Addams Family*

46. Opposite of ecto-

47. Blvds.

49. Day divs.

Solution on Page 280

ACROSS

1. Hems and ___
5. Merry month
8. Sugar container
12. Provo's state
13. Glacier's composition
14. "If you ask me," in textspeak
15. Bigger than big
16. Junior's junior
18. Brussels is its cap.
20. ___-Ida (frozen potato brand)
21. Needle-bearing trees
23. Infield covers
28. Degree held by many univ. professors
31. Speech impediment
33. ___-dish pizza
34. Main arteries
36. Laundry worker
38. Joel or Ethan of film
39. *Citizen* ___
41. Take a stab at
42. "Cut off your nose to ___ your face"
44. Docs prescribe them
46. Good blackjack card
48. Small dent
51. Poe story, "The ___ Heart"
56. The Beach Boys' "___ Vibrations"
58. Gallows reprieve
59. Opener for two tins?
60. Posterior
61. Put blacktop on
62. "Just a ___"
63. Pony's gait

DOWN

1. "Come again?"
2. "Three men in ___"
3. Worker's pay
4. Bookcase part
5. Russian plane
6. Crossword direction
7. Anniversary unit
8. Bit of eBay action
9. Meditation syllables
10. Sci-fi's *Doctor* ___
11. *Man of a Thousand Faces* Chaney
17. Butterfly-catching device
19. ___ monster (large lizard)
22. Insurer's exposure
24. Uproar
25. What homeowners don't have to pay
26. Jury member
27. Agile for one's age
28. Campaign funders, for short
29. Hula ___
30. Eins + zwei
32. Conifer with needles

35. Explosive stuff

37. Comedian Foxx

40. Aviator Earhart

43. Erode, with "away"

45. A ___ for sore eyes

47. Apple carrier

49. Black: Fr.

50. ___ farther (stop)

51. Baking soda meas.

52. Approximate landing hr.

53. Washroom: abbr.

54. Basic cleaner

55. Wrap up

57. Banned bug killer

Solution on Page 281

ACROSS

1. In the ___ of luxury
4. 100 cts.
7. Touches
12. Sit-ups strengthen them
13. Exiled Amin
14. Stalin's predecessor
15. Susan of *The Partridge Family*
16. Govt. property overseer
17. Sing like a bird
18. Don't have
20. Online journal
22. Moral precept
24. Part of UNLV
25. Gas additive letters
28. Inmate who's never getting out
30. Fruit-filled dessert
31. Took long steps
34. Available to rent
37. Instant lawn
38. Dog's restraint
40. Once existed
41. Negative prefix
42. *Green Eggs and Ham* author
46. Times New Roman, e.g.
47. Fly like a butterfly
48. Become narrower
51. Dorothy's aunt and others
54. Lao ___ (Chinese philosopher)
55. Uses a towel
56. ___ v. *Wade* (landmark decision)
57. Dream letters
58. No longer fresh
59. Mother hog
60. Nile cobra

DOWN

1. Soup server
2. "My Heart Skips ___"
3. ___ out (intimidate)
4. Archaeological site
5. Has too much of a bad thing
6. On the hook
7. Voices above tenors
8. Arctic floater
9. Prefix with cycle
10. Michael Jackson's "Don't Stop ___ You Get Enough"
11. NBC sketch show
19. Prefix with hertz
21. Insect stage
23. El ___ (Spanish hero)
25. Restorative resort
26. Malleable metal
27. Stroke gently
29. Serious offender
31. U-turn from NNE
32. Suit ___ tee
33. Country rtes.
35. Braying beast

36. Kitchen VIP

39. Keys in, as data

41. Like Leif Erikson

43. The "U" of UHF

44. Small, medium, and large

45. Baffle

46. Grope

48. QB's successes

49. Gallery offering

50. Zadora of *Butterfly*

52. Cow's comment

53. Fix a seam, e.g.

Solution on Page 281

ACROSS

1. Oddly amusing
6. Disney World attractions
11. Miniature
12. Smitten one
14. Kind of food or group
15. Strong-arm
16. Hillary Clinton, ___ Rodham
17. Phony
19. "…a man ___ mouse?"
20. Rocky outcropping
22. Hi-___ image
23. ___ Scott Decision (1857)
24. Where salt and fresh water mix
26. Fine rains
27. Center of a hurricane
28. Hollywood's Howard
29. Lower in public estimation
32. Bucharest's land
36. Falls behind
37. Picnic pest
38. ___ Christian Andersen
39. Suffix with Benedict
40. "___ Mommy Kissing Santa Claus"
42. Sound of disappointment
43. Bicycle for two
46. South Seas getaway
48. Like early audiobooks
49. 7-___

50. Syrian leader
51. Hibernation

DOWN

1. Dissuades
2. Prepare leftovers
3. Have the title to
4. Explorer Erikson
5. Spy novelist John
6. Indy 500 and others
7. Altar affirmation
8. Female deer
9. Goofs
10. Confidential matter
11. Parts of British pounds
13. Curls up with a book
18. Door opener
21. Twenty questions attempt
23. Entertainer Shore
25. Favorable vote
26. Pop's partner
28. Revolves
29. Samuel on the Supreme Court
30. Monkey treat
31. Insurance sellers
32. Hosp. workers
33. Original inhabitant
34. Arched foot part
35. Invite to enter

PUZZLE 95

37. Pointed a pistol

41. China has a Great one

44. ___ *Rheingold*

45. Govt. pollution watchdog

47. Part of a giggle

Solution on Page 281

Puzzles • 201

ACROSS

1. Baby bear
4. Fire starter
9. Step up from dial-up
12. Fri. preceder
13. Des Moines native
14. ___ out (just manage)
15. Place to get stuck
16. "___ say more?"
17. Ungentlemanly sort
18. ___ apso (dog breed)
20. To's partner
22. ___ the ground running
24. Within reach
27. Invasion date
30. Actress Gardner
32. Price of a ride
33. Celestial sphere
34. "Cry ___ River"
35. Freight weight
36. Something to shake with
38. And so on, briefly
39. Morning moistures
40. On the train
42. Trident-shaped Greek letter
44. Baseball hitting stat
45. Groups of cattle
49. Thanksgiving tuber
51. Musical pace
55. Over there, old-style
56. Dam-building org.
57. Hot coal
58. Storekeeper on *The Simpsons*
59. California's Marina ___ Rey
60. Get the ball rolling
61. Kan. neighbor

DOWN

1. Bottom-row PC key
2. Slangy denial
3. "Life is ___ dream"
4. Mideast peninsula
5. Edgar Allan ___
6. Impress greatly
7. Half a diam.
8. "Mack the ___"
9. Adorn
10. Some Caribbean music
11. Held first place
19. Introverted
21. Brit. flying group
23. Domesticated
24. Civil rights org.
25. Furrowed part of the head
26. Deep urges
27. Capital of Qatar
28. Lacking color
29. Not what you'd expect
31. Ex-GI
37. Small amount, as of hair cream

39. Six-sided roller
41. Religious ceremonies
43. Brief
46. Tatum's dad
47. Narc's seizure
48. Rudely overlook
49. Since Jan. 1, in financials

50. "___ Maria"
52. CPR specialist
53. Bus. deg.
54. MPH middle

Solution on Page 281

ACROSS

1. Easy letters?
4. ADA member
7. "Honor ___ father and…"
10. Alternatives to pumpernickels
12. Not safe, on the diamond
13. When repeated, a child's train
14. "___ on truckin'"
15. ___ good job (perform well): 2 wds.
16. Long and lean
17. Captains' records
19. Burn slightly
20. Outflow's opposite
23. 60 secs.
24. Puts into piles
25. Hardly ever
28. ___-night doubleheader
29. Solar system center
30. "Am ___ time?"
32. Few and far between
35. *The Treasure of the Sierra* ___
37. "Vamoose!"
38. Had a hunch
39. Sat in neutral
42. Hat fabric
43. Flipped thing
44. Kook
45. Giant-screen theater
49. Retained
50. Bud
51. Actress Blanchett
52. Decade divs.
53. *The Fountainhead* writer Rand
54. Part of FWIW

DOWN

1. Noah's construction
2. "See ya!"
3. Middling mark
4. Jump out of the way
5. Couples
6. RR depot
7. Comparison word
8. ___ Kong (Chinese port)
9. Oxen connector
11. Water balloon impact sound
13. "Crazy" singer Patsy
18. Approves, briefly
19. Title for a knight
20. Suffix for novel or violin
21. "___ as good a time as any"
22. Fall over one's feet
23. Isle of ___
25. Feel regret over
26. Jar covers
27. Days long past
29. Mach+ jet
31. Actor Beatty
33. FBI operative

34. Cleansed (of)

35. *Braveheart* star Gibson

36. Playful trick

38. ___ Hall (New Jersey university)

39. Disgusting

40. Idler's opposite

41. They're kissable

42. Intense anger

44. Michael Jordan's org.

46. ___ tai (cocktail)

47. Ma Bell

48. Illiterates' marks

Solution on Page 282

ACROSS

1. Drugstore chain
4. Stamp for an incoming pkg.
8. Use an eggbeater
12. Almost empty
13. Opposite of dry, as hair
14. Lyricist Lorenz
15. "Ain't ___ shame?"
16. Loser at the dice table
18. ___ dish (lab container)
20. "I haven't a thing to ___!"
21. Like many seniors: abbr.
23. Do you understand?
27. ___ and wherefores
30. Sweep under the rug
33. Grp. that entertains troops
34. Shade
35. Enjoy the taste of
36. Keg attachment
37. None's opposite
38. Dockside platform
39. Dolls' companions
40. Oklahoma's second-largest city
42. Opposite of nay
44. Prepare presents
47. Photo book
51. School terms
55. Card game akin to crazy eights
56. Alka-Seltzer sound
57. Oil of ___

58. *Blame It On* ___ (Caine comedy)
59. Punch ingredient?
60. Actress Catherine ___-Jones
61. Beetle Bailey's rank: abbr.

DOWN

1. Cut out, as coupons
2. Cast a ballot
3. Police team acronym
4. TV host O'Donnell
5. "A," in Austria
6. Cat's scratcher
7. TV's Dick Van ___
8. "...___ angels fear to tread"
9. Bale contents
10. Fury
11. Barnum and 109, e.g.
17. Raring to go
19. B&O and Union Pacific
22. Pad ___ (noodle dish)
24. Ballet skirt
25. "Do as ___, not…"
26. Best toys in the whirl?
27. One of the five W's
28. Streaming video giant
29. Tarzan's is famous
31. "___ been to the mountaintop": King
32. Hunky-___
35. Practices in the ring

39. Guy's mate

41. Cleaned the floor

43. High mark with low effort

45. Completely, after "from"

46. Brazilian soccer star

48. Pat baby on the back

49. Prof.'s employer

50. No longer worth debating

51. Letters on a Coppertone bottle

52. Cotton gin inventor Whitney

53. Rapper ___ Def

54. Pied Piper follower

Solution on Page 282

ACROSS

1. Encountered
4. Prefix with dermal
7. Like molasses
11. "A long time ___ in a galaxy far, far away…"
12. Indian flatbreads
14. Pig's sound
15. Break, as a balloon
16. Yahtzee pieces
17. Tracks in mud
18. Give the cold shoulder
20. Back, on a ship
22. Will of *The Waltons*
23. Stern and Newton
26. ___ Remus
27. Rocket scientist Wernher ___ Braun
28. Experimentation station
30. Old MacDonald's place
31. Snorkeling accessory
32. Hardly tanned
33. Be in the hole
34. Dr. of hip-hop
35. Wait on
36. Remained
38. Auto brand
39. "Zip-A-___-Doo-Dah"
40. Job benefit
41. Neighbor of Niger
44. James Brown's genre
46. Superman symbol
49. Yep's opposite
50. Above average in height
51. Teachers' union, in brief
52. Cornhusker St.
53. Spider's prey
54. Former *Grand Ole Opry* network

DOWN

1. Cartographer's creation
2. Id companion
3. Highly classified
4. Hang in there
5. "No ___, no gain"
6. Corp. abbr.
7. Somewhat, informally
8. Actress Lucy
9. Canadian prov.
10. Calendar rows: abbr.
13. Spring or summer
19. Captain's place
21. Ceiling spinner
22. Chews like a beaver
23. Like some college walls
24. Superman's alter ego
25. Burn balm
26. ET's ride
29. Hive occupant
31. Least restrained

32. Fruit cocktail fruit

34. Redhead maker

35. Odoriferous

37. Venomous snake

40. Yank

41. Atlanta's ___ Center

42. Tough row to ___

43. NYPD alert

45. Clumsy fellow

47. Rep.'s counterpart

48. ___ Bernardino

Solution on Page 282

ACROSS

1. Sandwich letters
4. Tennis great Monica
9. Boston Red ___
12. Mauna ___ (Hawaiian volcano)
13. Political influence
14. "Either he goes ___ go!"
15. Piece of sound equipment
16. Houston baseballer
17. Med. diagnostic tool
18. Pesto herb
20. CIA Cold War counterpart
22. Rebel Turner
24. Lack
27. "___ Sorry Now?"
30. Mature, as wine
32. Richard of *American Gigolo*
33. 007 creator Fleming
34. Sweetie
35. Basketball net holder
36. Emulated Pinocchio
38. Horse's morsel
39. Mongolian desert
40. Plaza Hotel girl of fiction
42. Telepathic letters
44. Extreme degree
45. Blue Ribbon beer brewer
49. Mil. address
51. Playing marble
55. From ___ Z (completely)
56. Solo in Star Wars
57. Baseball great Pee Wee
58. On the ___ (at large)
59. Feminine pronoun
60. Argue a case
61. Lots of oz.

DOWN

1. Spill the beans
2. ___ Linda, California
3. Bugler's evening call
4. Milan's La ___
5. Pro golfer Ernie
6. Parking area
7. Continental abbr.
8. Stir up and feed, as a fire
9. Hat dance hat
10. Bobby of hockey
11. Noon, on a sundial
19. Shoo-___ (sure winners)
21. Comic's bit
23. Lake on the California-Nevada border
24. Al ___ (pasta style)
25. Chi-town paper, with "the"
26. Prefix meaning "half"
27. ___ E. Coyote
28. Signal, as a cab
29. Mano a mano
31. ___ few rounds (spar)

37. Dah's partner

39. 4.0 is a great one: abbr.

41. Pointy

43. Swiftness

46. Event attended by Cinderella

47. Seize with a toothpick

48. *Uncle ___ Cabin*

49. Sounds of relief

50. Oom___ band

52. Hairdo stiffener

53. "How about that!"

54. *Happiness ___ Warm Puppy*

Solution on Page 282

ACROSS

1. Gov't air-safety org.
4. Corp. honcho
7. Runs for exercise
11. AOL or MSN: abbr.
12. "Barbara ___" (Beach Boys classic)
13. 3:1 or 7:2, e.g.
14. Just enough to wet the lips
15. Tic-toe connection
16. Spacek of *Carrie*
17. Twain portrayer Holbrook
18. Head-and-shoulders sculpture
20. Not used
22. Serve to be re-served
23. Putter's target
26. "Honest" presidential nickname
28. Lower in value
31. Actress Roberts
34. Vice ___ (conversely)
35. Christie of mystery
37. Campbell's container
38. Philosopher's question
39. Dent or scratch
41. Welby and Kildare: abbr.
44. ___ off (hockey opener)
45. Choose to participate, with "in"
47. Home of Arizona State
51. Dodge truck
53. Bygone Russian space station
54. Napoleon's fate
55. "What am ___ do?"
56. Shar-___ (wrinkly dog)
57. Art ___: geometric style
58. Dawn droplets
59. ___-mo (instant replay feature)

DOWN

1. Ichthyologist's study
2. From the East
3. Macintosh maker
4. Mouse chaser
5. Give power to
6. Perfectly timed
7. ___ alai
8. Tiebreaker rounds: abbr.
9. USO audience
10. Tofu base
13. Queue after Q
19. Regular: abbr.
21. Word repeated before "Don't tell me!"
23. Roadster
24. Ship letters
25. Little green veggie
27. Scrooge's cry
29. *Green Acres* star Gabor
30. Curve
31. Uppercut's target
32. "That's horrid!"
33. "Now I ___ me down…"

212

36. "Today I ___ man" (bar mitzvah phrase)

37. Bring into existence

40. Bitterly pungent

42. Frolics

43. Long-winded sales pitch

44. Broker's charge

46. Quartet, after a defection

47. *Nightline* host Koppel

48. Common file name extension

49. Open ___ night

50. Arafat's group: abbr.

52. Cut the grass

Solution on Page 283

ACROSS

1. They rank below capts.
4. Thurman of film
7. Junk bond rating
10. Salad bowl wood
12. Mom's girl
13. Chunk of concrete
14. Cold cuts purveyor
15. Young Darth Vader's nickname
16. Model's stance
17. Boost
19. "Peter, Peter, Pumpkin ___"
20. Parsley portion
23. Newspaper sales fig.
25. Texas battle site of 1836
26. Cantankerous
29. Prefix with bytes or bucks
30. Genetic code letters
31. Without feeling
33. Damaged, as a fender
35. Joe of *GoodFellas*
36. Guitarist Hendrix
37. Get-well program
38. "___ a dark and stormy night…"
41. ___ on (trampled)
43. Superhero with a hammer
44. Soccer Hall of Famer Hamm
45. Mascara target
49. Worst possible test score
50. Election mo.
51. Proctored event
52. Suffix with meth- or eth-
53. ___-in-a-million (rare)
54. *The Name of the Rose* author
    Umberto

DOWN

1. Co. alternative
2. Golf ball raiser
3. *My Gal* ___
4. Mil. fliers
5. Perfect shape, to a collector
6. "___ always say…"
7. Coagulate, as blood
8. Part of a judge's docket
9. Trucker with a transmitter
11. Africa's highest peak
13. Seattle landmark
18. "Where did ___ wrong?"
19. Suffix for southeast
20. Patriotic uncle
21. Appealed earnestly
22. All the ___ (wildly popular)
24. Roth plan, for one
27. ___-hour traffic
28. Community gym site
30. Rep. foe
32. Apparel for a young diner
34. "___ the season…"
35. Golf lesson provider

PUZZLE 102

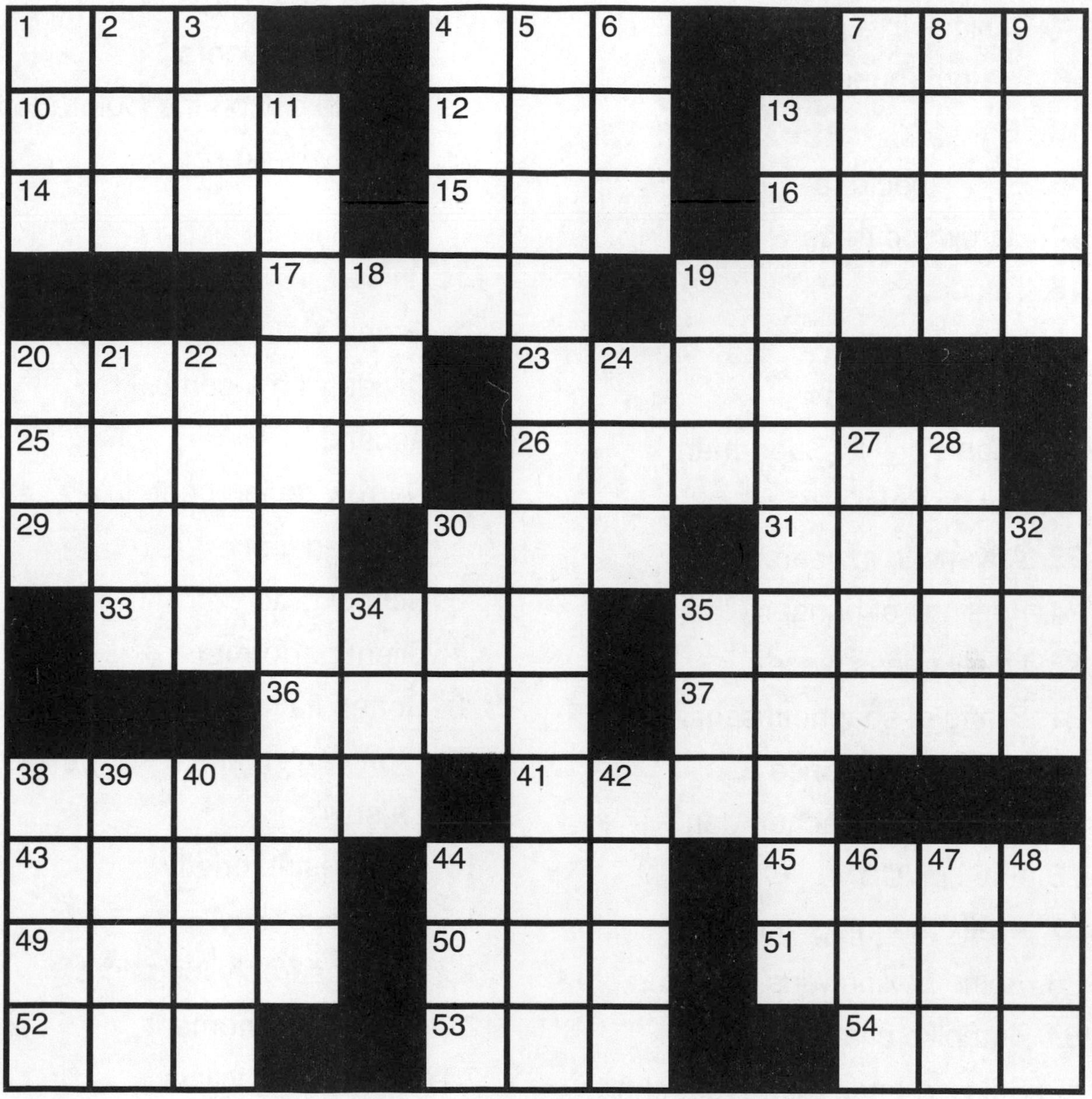

38. Chichen ___ (Mayan ruins)
39. "That was ___…"
40. Sported
42. Enthusiastic review
44. L–P connection
46. Felling tool
47. Possum's pouch
48. Patient-care grp.

Solution on Page 283

ACROSS

1. Class for EMTs
4. Did laps in a pool
8. ___ out (apportion)
12. "Bali ___"
13. E. ___ bacteria
14. Hardwood trees
15. Tax dept.
16. E pluribus ___
17. Gator's cousin
18. "Man of ___" (Superman)
20. Net material
22. Advanced in years
24. Feelings of hunger
28. Lowly chess piece
31. Brand of spaghetti sauce
34. Backrub response
35. "Son ___ Preacher Man"
36. The I in ICBM
37. Prefix meaning "three"
38. Some boxing wins, for short
39. Turnpike charge
40. Scissorhands portrayer Johnny
41. Be
43. Downhearted
45. Black-___ Susan
48. Changed the decor of
52. 5,280 feet
55. "Just do it" sloganeer
57. Beatle bride Yoko
58. Corner piece in chess
59. Blood vessel
60. Super Bowl org.
61. Butter containers
62. Arizona city on the Colorado River
63. Wobbly walker

DOWN

1. Greek X's
2. Divide with a comb
3. Ascend
4. Narrow racing boat
5. Finished first
6. School grad
7. Silent performer
8. Coffee flavor
9. "You can't make a silk purse out of a sow's ___"
10. Ring result, briefly
11. PC "oops" key
19. Immeasurably long time
21. ___-of-the-moment
23. Ian Fleming villain
25. Basketball's Archibald
26. *The World According to* ___
27. Use UPS, e.g.
28. ___ fun at (ridicule)
29. Sly as ___
30. "Now, where ___?"
32. Home of the Braves: abbr.
33. Hair goops

36. ___-bitty

40. JFK's predecessor

42. Tries to find

44. Sporting venue

46. Be jealous of

47. "Mon ___!"

49. "Stop it!"

50. Help desk offering, briefly

51. Oaf

52. Chain-wearing *A-Team* actor

53. Lendee's note

54. High tennis shot

56. Novak or Basinger

Solution on Page 283

ACROSS

1. Delivery docs, for short
4. Pt. of speech
7. Remnant
11. ___ and tuck
12. Hen pen
14. Golf target
15. Like some stocks, for short
16. Fey or Turner
17. Radio switch
18. Justification
20. *Fresh Air* airer
22. London's land: abbr.
23. Take down a notch
27. Candidate lists
30. Rouse
31. Coll. helpers
32. Young feller
33. Capital of Turkey
37. Yearly records
40. Approached
41. Yank's war foe
42. Ill. neighbor
43. Break for students
47. Univ. awards
50. "___ it my way"
52. Tiny criticism
53. Extra-wide shoe size
54. Use a piggy bank
55. Have a bawl
56. Ones ranked above cpls.
57. "___ give you the shirt off his back"
58. Superman archvillain Luthor

DOWN

1. ___ about (roughly)
2. Angler's quest
3. Pet advocacy org.
4. Start of a play
5. Goings-on
6. Rocker Bon Jovi
7. TV's ___ & *Greg*
8. CD follower
9. Assistant to Santa
10. Precious stone
13. Bamboo eater
19. Collection of like items
21. Bench with a back
24. Tulsa's state: abbr.
25. Greenish blue
26. Brings to a halt
27. Getz or Kenton
28. Superman's Lois
29. "May I ___ silly question?"
34. Comes up
35. Stimpy's canine pal
36. ___ Ababa, Ethiopia
37. Depart's opposite
38. Couldn't do without

39. "The peacock network"

44. Abbr. on a business letter

45. Foal's father

46. River of the underworld

47. ___ Plaines

48. Brain wave reading: abbr.

49. "___ real!"

51. "Zip-a-Dee-Doo-___"

Solution on Page 283

ACROSS

1. Voyage with Captain Kirk
5. Ask for alms
8. *Return of the Jedi* creature
12. Cabbagelike vegetable
13. Glacial
14. "___ help you?"
15. Finished
16. Mexican food staple
18. "...not always what they ___"
19. Bank transaction
20. Brainpower stats
23. Red vegetables
27. Hit, as flies
31. Stallion's mate
32. Golf target
33. Winter neckwear
36. Use an oar
37. ___ to say (implying)
39. Space creatures, maybe
41. Glass fragment
43. A–E connection
44. New Age energy field
47. "Highway to Hell" band
51. Mind readers
55. ___ bargain
56. It might make you say "Aha!"
57. Kind of shot
58. Like Bunyan's tales
59. Restaurant valet's income
60. Margarine container
61. Triathlon leg

DOWN

1. Boxing wins, for short
2. Glowing review
3. Gen. Robert ___
4. Muppet frog
5. Took the bait
6. Earth Day subj.
7. Greek sandwich
8. *8 Mile* rapper
9. ___mart (retail chain)
10. Olive ___
11. Sedona maker
17. It's run up and then settled
21. Oil amts.
22. "Wait a ___!"
24. Bring in, as a salary
25. Relaxed running pace
26. Makes clothes
27. Hot tubs
28. Do the laundry
29. Diva's solo
30. Beaver's project
34. Cause friction
35. US commerce watchdog
38. Disorderly disturbance
40. Adjusts to fit

42. Comment made while slapping the forehead
45. Break in friendly relations
46. Civil rights org.
48. Crab's grabber
49. Place to get a Reuben
50. Storm preceder

51. Cherry seed
52. Reagan-era mil. program
53. "Uh-huh"
54. Fill-in

Solution on Page 284

ACROSS

1. ___ Pérignon champagne
4. The "A" of IRA: abbr.
8. After-hours money sources, for short
12. Wrigley Field flora
13. Dove sounds
14. Infamous Roman emperor
15. Fox's home
16. Ticker-___ parade
17. Political cartoonist Thomas
18. Bound by routine
20. Remove the fat from
22. Undergrad degs.
23. Nap in Oaxaca
26. Thrash about
29. Tent pin
30. Apex
31. Morays and congers
32. Faux ___ (social slip-up)
33. Tenant's monthly check
34. Mix or Cruise
35. ___ Bartlet, president on *The West Wing*
36. Skin openings
37. Fill with love
39. Morse code character
40. Turndowns
41. Cookbook entry
45. ___ *a Teenage Werewolf*
47. "Make the most ___"
49. Pro ___ (for now)
50. Composer Johann Sebastian
51. ___-do-well
52. Intel product, briefly
53. Retailer's goods: abbr.
54. Cockeyed
55. "For ___ a jolly…"

DOWN

1. "What ___ do to deserve this?"
2. Baking chamber
3. Talking bird
4. Not just imagined
5. Checkroom items
6. Officer of the peace
7. Dangerous African flies
8. Comics orphan
9. Trucker in a union
10. ___ Butterworth's
11. Soused sort
19. Sluggers' stats
21. Fix illegally
24. Musical pitch
25. Places for rent: abbr.
26. Gala gathering
27. Trotsky or Uris
28. Annually published fact books
29. Shoulder enhancer
32. ___ non grata

33. Univ. military program

35. Coffee, in slang

36. Limericks and sonnets

38. Israeli leader Dayan

39. Not as moist

42. Result of a mosquito bite

43. Cartoon skunk Le Pew

44. Flightless flock

45. Big name in early PCs

46. Roll of bills

48. Handful

Solution on Page 284

ACROSS

1. Intl. clock standard
4. Puts a question to
8. Prescriptions, for short
12. Singer Orbison
13. Ballerina's knee bend
14. Korea's continent
15. Type
16. Fragrant wood
17. Free ticket, for short
18. Become more intense
20. Amount in a whiskey glass
22. Dustcloth
23. Go back on one's word
26. Peter the pepper picker
29. Tina of *30 Rock*
30. Drop of golden sun
31. "Sad to say…"
32. Divining device
33. ___ of passage
34. Toe count
35. Take more than one's share of
36. Walks back and forth
37. Gems
39. It's north of Okla.
40. Where the Vatican is
41. Acid neutralizer
45. Wharton degs.
47. Ripped apart
49. Rifle or revolver
50. Actress Moore of *Ghost*
51. Rolaids competitor
52. Wood used for wine barrels
53. The sun, e.g.
54. Smell ___ (be leery)
55. Fellow

DOWN

1. Graph paper pattern
2. Burrowing mammal
3. Youngster
4. Come into view
5. Injured arm support
6. Reunion folks
7. Goes ballistic
8. City of central Georgia
9. Shrouded in mystery
10. Poorly lit
11. Maple output
19. JFK or LBJ
21. Attention-getting shout
24. Fence opening
25. Peepers
26. ___ down (frisks)
27. "Before ___ you go…"
28. Scenic view
29. Driving hazard
32. ___ Stone (hieroglyphics key)
33. ___ and file
35. Anti-fray border

224

36. Lightest-colored

38. Military denial

39. Destiny, in Buddhism

42. Wide-eyed

43. Cookout in Honolulu

44. Like printers' fingers

45. Hosp. workers

46. Gamble

48. "Give us this day ___ daily bread"

Solution on Page 284

ACROSS

1. 1996 candidate Dole
4. In doubt
8. Tanner's tub
11. Tiny battery size
13. Absolutely positive
14. Grammy winner Winehouse
15. ___ Reaper
16. Kazan who directed *On the Waterfront*
17. ChapStick target
18. Beach drier
20. Stockholm native
22. Lock horns
24. Chose, with "for"
26. Japanese currency
27. ___ Romeo (sports car)
29. Prong of a fork
32. Vicious or Caesar
33. Demi or Dudley
35. End of many URLs
36. Job to do
38. Inst. of higher learning
39. Allen of *Home Improvement*
40. Witty Oscar
42. University in Atlanta
44. Reprove
46. Submarine detector
48. Scorching
49. Cry from the pews

51. Fixes illegally
54. Bar code
55. Surrealist Salvador
56. "Please?"
57. "Doesn't excite me"
58. Downy
59. Habit wearer

DOWN

1. "Paper or plastic?" item
2. Canoe propeller
3. Unscrupulous sales tactic
4. Fortune-teller's start
5. Conceited
6. Sat. preceder
7. Dough leavener
8. College commencement speaker
9. In the thick of
10. Use a Smith-Corona
12. Andy's pal on old radio
19. "Pow!"
21. Soaked
22. Bodily sac
23. Han Solo's love
25. ___-mutuel (form of betting)
28. Earsplitting
30. Roulette color
31. Television award
34. Divisible by two
37. Young goat

226

41. Clues, to a detective

43. Cleopatra's love ___ Antony

44. Pal

45. Despair's opposite

47. "Don't bet ___!"

50. ___ Tse-tung

52. Homophone for new

53. One of the seven deadlies

Solution on Page 284

ACROSS

1. Elec. usage measure
4. Having what it takes
8. Recipe abbr.
12. Actress Myrna
13. Carpentry fastener
14. Wash-and-___
15. *The ___ Squad* of '60s–'70s TV
16. Just twiddling one's thumbs
17. On pins and needles
18. Suffix with Oktober
20. Feed lines to
22. Seniors' org.
25. Get used (to)
29. Sound of astonishment
32. "Is there ___ against that?"
34. Soap unit
35. Tavern mugfuls
36. Postgrad degs.
37. Trifling
38. At this moment
39. "Sheesh, ___ you read?"
40. "That ___ it should be"
41. Birthplace of Columbus
43. Any second now
45. Grilling, for short
47. Talk show host Dr. ___
50. Actor Dick Van ___
53. Ebb or neap
56. Fish-and-chips fish
58. Baby kangaroo
59. What bodybuilders pump
60. Ghost's greeting
61. Solar-system centers
62. UPS deliveries
63. Speedometer letters

DOWN

1. Dutch airline
2. St. Bernard's bark
3. Jekyll's counterpart
4. Singer Baker
5. Like Leroy Brown
6. Capp's Abner
7. Power co. product
8. Jacket material
9. Fourposter, e.g.
10. Drop in the middle
11. Use a crowbar
19. Drains
21. Detroit labor org.
23. "___ Lama Ding Dong"
24. Thinks ahead
26. Beame and Burrows
27. Trooper prefix
28. Uno plus dos
29. Crips or Bloods
30. Burn balm
31. ___ up (in the bag)
33. Regarding, in a memo
37. Ho Chi ___ City

39. Car for hire

42. Follows the leader

44. Uncorks

46. Swab brand

48. Mil. weapon that can cross an ocean

49. Roller coaster feature

50. Dance club VIPs

51. "___ Are My Sunshine"

52. 2016 Hall of Fame inductee ___ Griffey Jr.

54. Annoy

55. Fido, for one

57. Play-___ (kids' clay)

Solution on Page 285

ACROSS

1. *The Joy Luck Club* writer Tan
4. "Against All ___"
8. *Dark Angel* star Jessica
12. Keanu's *The Matrix* role
13. Red vegetable
14. Sticky stuff
15. Calendar square
16. "For the life ___..."
17. Prego rival
18. Rock
20. "___ is me!"
22. Scandinavian capital
25. Jokes
29. Skin problem
32. Conceited people have big ones
34. Color
35. Hockey score
36. Nightmare street of film
37. NY neighbor
38. Paranormal ability, for short
39. Chirpy bird
40. Take notice
41. Look without blinking
43. Widespread
45. Recede, as the tide
47. SeaWorld performers
51. Therefore
54. Smartphone downloads
57. Little rascal
58. It holds a bunch
59. Lipton and Twinings, e.g.
60. Buttonless shirt
61. Part of GPS: abbr.
62. Bargain event
63. Computer key

DOWN

1. & & &
2. Vegetarian's no-no
3. Toy on a string
4. Woodwind instruments
5. Rock's ___ Leppard
6. Rep.'s opponent
7. Fret (over)
8. Shake on it
9. Mauna ___ (brand of macadamia nuts)
10. Peat source
11. Kwik-E-Mart clerk on *The Simpsons*
19. Christmas song
21. IHOP beverages
23. Lustful look
24. Girl watcher, perhaps
26. Nike product
27. Something to whistle
28. Drop in the mail
29. Ripens, as cheese
30. Amount to pay
31. California wine county
33. Prefix with bus or potent

PUZZLE 110

37. Sonny's partner, once
39. World Wide ___
42. Put back to zero, as a tripmeter
44. *All That Jazz* choreographer Bob
46. Flying mammals
48. Issue a ticket to
49. Spy Aldrich
50. Job detail, briefly
51. Idiot boxes
52. Farm bale
53. Naval letters
55. Round green veggie
56. Chum

Solution on Page 285

ACROSS

1. Tiny
4. Openings
8. Bed with bars
12. Battery size
13. Keep ___ profile
14. "___ comes trouble!"
15. Many months: abbr.
16. "___ penny, pick it up…"
17. Work without ___ (take risks)
18. Respond to seeing red?
20. Negatives
22. "Hey, you!"
25. Rule the kingdom
29. Sit for a photo
32. Erie or Huron
34. "…good witch ___ bad witch?"
35. Certain look-alike
38. Tiny Dickens boy
39. ___-Eaters (shoe inserts)
40. Honey Bunches of ___
41. Bank robber's job
43. Smelting waste
45. Part of UCLA
47. Bruce Springsteen, with "The"
50. "…can't believe ___ the whole thing!"
53. Arthur ___ Stadium
56. "___ a real nowhere man…"
58. Just ___ (not much)
59. In the ___ breath (almost simultaneously)
60. "I Got Rhythm" lyricist Gershwin
61. Haves and have-___
62. Where to drop a coin
63. Afternoon snooze

DOWN

1. Route
2. What the walls have, they say
3. Toward the sunrise
4. Sounds of shock
5. Taproom order
6. "Once upon a midnight dreary" writer
7. Graceful bird
8. Run after
9. Stimpy's sidekick
10. Wrath
11. Take the odds
19. Unseal
21. Baseball's Hershiser
23. Glided
24. Mexican snacks
26. Political caucus state
27. Sandpaper coating
28. Indian restaurant breads
29. Kind of helmet in safari films
30. Garfield's canine pal
31. 18-wheeler
33. Bush adviser Rove
36. Dog on the Yellow Brick Road

37. Not for here

42. Snow sliders

44. Red as ___

46. Bratty talk

48. ___ splints (jogger's woe)

49. Antitoxins

50. Novelist Fleming

51. ___ Z

52. Rat-a-___

54. "I've got a mule, her name is ___"

55. Patient-care grp.

57. Tree juice

Solution on Page 285

ACROSS

1. ___ Pan Alley
4. Lovers' quarrel
8. TV monitoring grp.
11. Japanese soup noodles
13. Bread for gyros
14. British john
15. *Animal House* garb
16. Phone abbr.
17. *The Ice Storm* director Lee
18. Work wk. start
20. Pictures on a screen
22. Cutting rays
25. Over-the-hill horse
26. Fore's opposite
27. Cowboy Rogers
29. Gemstone measure
33. Brother of Abel
35. New Deal agcy.
37. Not great, but not awful either
38. Dropped fly ball, e.g.
40. Pose, as a question
42. Cobbler's tool
43. "Ready, ___, go!"
45. Appeared to be
47. Playwright O'Neill
50. What a quill may be dipped in
51. You-know-___
52. Tongue-clicking sounds
54. ___ A Sketch: drawing toy
58. Ger. continent
59. Came down to earth
60. "Scat, cat!"
61. "Steady as ___ goes"
62. Lassies' partners
63. Ref's relative

DOWN

1. Egyptian boy king
2. Words before "You may kiss the bride"
3. Eggy drink
4. "And now a word from our ___"
5. Spot on a playing card
6. Dined at home
7. Airport surface
8. Old Glory, for one
9. Ice cream holder
10. Gear teeth
12. Driver's license datum
19. Hockey Hall of Famer Bobby
21. "Jumpin' Jack Flash, it's ___" (1968 lyric)
22. Valentine decoration
23. "They worshipped from ___"
24. Blend
28. Vote of support
30. Wander about
31. "…___ forgive those who trespass…"
32. Tattled

34. Scent detector

36. Lends a hand

39. Alamo offering

41. *Jeopardy!* whiz Jennings

44. Croatian-born physicist Nikola

46. ___ out: makes do

47. Lambs' ma'ams

48. "Not gonna happen"

49. Clinton's veep

53. *The Karate* ___ (1984)

55. Day after Wed.

56. Common URL ender

57. Short flight

Solution on Page 285

ACROSS

1. Antitrust agcy.
4. Seek the affection of
7. Big swallow
11. 401(k) alternatives
13. Former California fort
14. "Alas!"
15. Newcastle's river
16. Completely free
17. Boor
18. Where the deer and the antelope play
20. Russia's Itar-___ news agency
21. Turn the ___ cheek
24. Cosby show
26. Rice-___ ("The San Francisco Treat")
27. Ultimate in degree
28. Chinese cooking vessel
31. Ancient Roman robes
32. Chicago terminal
34. "Killing Me Softly with ___ Song"
35. Bill at the bar
38. One over par
39. Bye-bye, in Brighton
40. Agenda details
41. White as a ghost
44. ___ a time (individually)
46. Ever and ___
47. Former Russian space station
48. Ballpark arbiters
52. *Saturday Night Live* segment
53. Any doctrine
54. Lisa Simpson's brother
55. Makes leather
56. "___-ching!" (cash register noise)
57. "___ Light Up My Life"

DOWN

1. Like a fiddle?
2. Word repeated after "If at first you don't succeed"
3. Fire
4. Like secondhand clothing
5. Starting point
6. Most bizarre
7. Like pretzels
8. Horse-stopping exclamation
9. Radio host Don
10. "Smoke ___ in Your Eyes"
12. Tennis star Williams
19. Competitor of Capitol and Epic
21. Solemn promise
22. *Star Trek: TNG* counselor Deanna
23. Swine
25. Fear
28. Salary
29. Utah city near Provo
30. Lock openers
33. Sociable soaking spot

236

PUZZLE 113

36. Part of AEC
37. Send into exile
39. Camp shelters
41. It might be checkered
42. “Puppy Love” singer Paul
43. Cut of meat
45. Writer Bombeck
49. Memorial Day month
50. Tennis club instructor
51. Trio after R

Solution on Page 286

ACROSS

1. Submachine gun
4. Cable news source
7. Train track
11. Brown quickly
13. *Playboy* mogul, to pals
14. Mock words of understanding
15. Auntie of Broadway
16. "Wise" bird
17. Singer k.d.
18. Necklace fasteners
20. Borrowers' burdens
21. Freezing period
24. Apple tablet computers
27. Archaeological operation
28. Tit ___ tat
31. Opposite of all
32. Run for exercise
33. Role to play
34. Boo-hoo
35. ___ Four (Beatles)
36. Mississippi River transport
37. Puts up, as a tower
39. Valuable fur
43. Wanted felon
47. Prefix with distant or lateral
48. Former telecom giant
50. "Do I dare to ___ peach?"
51. Litter's littlest
52. Approving head shake
53. Chop ___
54. First, second, or third, on a diamond
55. Raises, as the ante
56. *The ___ Moines Register*

DOWN

1. Mil. branch
2. Eagerness
3. Simon and Garfunkel's "___ Rock"
4. Picked
5. Just minted
6. Steelers' org.
7. Rattling breath
8. Melville hero
9. "Winning ___ everything"
10. Fireplace fuel
12. Live (at)
19. Dell products
20. Temperature abbr.
22. Southwestern home material
23. Band booking
24. *Monsters, ___*
25. "___ favor, señor!"
26. "___ objections?"
28. Hardy's ___ *from the Madding Crowd*
29. Nonprofit website suffix
30. Motorist's way: abbr.
32. It holds the mayo

33. Uses glue

35. Lawyer's payment

36. A/C measure

38. Sorority members

39. Kosovo war participant

40. Color of water

41. Wiener holders

42. Low-calorie

44. Heap praise on

45. To ___ (perfectly)

46. ___ and Means Committee

48. Bearded grazer

49. Go one better

Solution on Page 286

ACROSS

1. Honest ___ (presidential moniker)
4. Runner's circuit
7. Roseanne, once
11. Butter slice
12. Stately shade trees
14. Fibber
15. Bit of horse feed
16. Perfume ingredient
17. The "A" in BA
18. Hospital fluid
20. Positive replies
22. 1040 org.
23. Falsehood
24. Actor Connery
27. Prohibition
28. Boxer nicknamed "The Greatest"
31. Murphy Brown portrayer
35. ___ a Wonderful Life
36. Screen siren West
37. Long, long time
38. Madam's partner
39. Taxpayer's ID
41. British biscuit
43. "Guilty" and "not guilty"
46. '60s NASA target
47. Eye irritation
49. Baglike structure
51. Like a bump on ___
52. Little ___ of Horrors
53. Doctors' org.
54. Putrefies
55. Toronto's loc.
56. Ore. clock setting

DOWN

1. GI's mail drop
2. Sheep cries
3. Suffix with kitchen or luncheon
4. Madagascar primate
5. Homecoming visitors
6. Parliament VIPs
7. Nonchalant
8. Suffix with concession
9. Charlie Brown's "Darn!"
10. Monopoly quartet: abbr.
13. Bygone space station
19. Melon throwaway
21. German "a"
24. Bio. or chem.
25. ___ one's words
26. Ques. response
27. Pollen collector
28. In the past
29. Dawson or Dykstra
30. Walk-___ (clients sans appointments)
32. "___ the Mood for Love"
33. Stroke lovingly
34. Descartes or Russo

38. Musical numbers

39. Watch covertly

40. Got some Z's

41. One-person performance

42. Crotchety oldster

44. Quickly: abbr.

45. Snead and Spade

46. Tarnish

48. However, informally

50. Panther or puma

Solution on Page 286

ACROSS

1. "We try harder" company
5. Brynner of *The Magnificent Seven*
8. Milk choice
12. Fender bender memento
13. Scannable mdse. bars
14. *The Diary of ___ Frank*
15. Luke Skywalker, for one
16. Chic, to Austin Powers
17. Vegetable soup bean
18. Custard dessert
20. Roadside stopover
21. Russian money
24. Rockers ___ Jovi
25. Actor Zimbalist Jr.
26. Short-legged hound
29. Bashful
30. Large
31. Vigor's partner
33. Speak sharply to
36. Harsh reflection
38. What cows chew
39. Group of experts
40. Piece of land
43. Conclude, with "up"
45. Chancellor von Bismarck
46. Prefix with light
47. *Iliad* setting
51. Reply to "Shall we?"
52. Command for Fido
53. Prefix meaning "eight"
54. Future atty.'s exam
55. Seoul-based automaker
56. Fill a suitcase

DOWN

1. Modifying word: abbr.
2. Neckline shape
3. Not Rep. or Dem.
4. Suppress
5. City WSW of Phoenix
6. Stratford-___-Avon
7. PC screen type
8. Beauty parlors
9. Make a sweater
10. "She Believes ___" (Kenny Rogers song)
11. Breakfast, lunch, or dinner
19. Moon lander, for short
20. Jan. and Feb.
21. ___ room
22. Sci-fi saucers
23. ___ Mawr College
24. Bellhop's burden
26. Drill attachment
27. Writer Hunter
28. Grow weary
30. Not behaving well
32. Singer Tormé
34. Confront boldly

35. Postpone, with "off"

36. Univ. transcript number

37. Portable computer

40. Driver's payment

41. Numbered rds.

42. Lead-in to girl

43. V-J Day ended it

44. Hayworth or Moreno

46. Sound uttered while shaking the head

48. "His Master's Voice" label

49. Where some stks. trade

50. Tibetan ox

Solution on Page 286

ACROSS

1. Raise crops
5. 24-hr. cash source
8. Queue after A
11. Like a raucous stadium crowd
13. *Back to the Future* actress Thompson
14. It's a boy
15. Take the role of
16. *The Joy Luck Club* author
17. Pig ___ poke
18. Tot's "piggies"
20. Wok-user's sauce
21. It may be glossed over
24. "Med" or "law" lead-in
25. NNW's reverse
26. Beaded calculator
29. 1-1 or 2-2, e.g.
31. Heredity carriers
32. Yielded
36. Cultural grant giver, for short
38. Covet
39. Hamelin pest
41. "Turn on, tune in, drop out" drug
43. *Grand Ole Opry* airer
44. Pro's opposite
45. Watkins ___, NY
47. Put two and two together
48. Bovine utterance
49. Takes five
54. Hawaiian necklace
55. ___-Magnon man
56. Danger signal
57. Adversary
58. Labor Day mo.
59. Soviet ballistic missile

DOWN

1. Air safety grp.
2. Pop fly's path
3. Spoil
4. Pasture sound
5. Change the hemline
6. Cups, saucers, etc.
7. Homo sapiens
8. Seventh heaven
9. Tippy craft
10. June 6, 1944
12. Q–U connection
19. Photo ___ (White House events)
21. Jet ___ (traveler's woe)
22. "When Will ___ Loved"
23. Pie holder
25. Lays eyes on
27. Gumball cost, once
28. "___ your head!"
30. Cubes in a tray
33. Telegraph signal
34. Long-winged sea eagle
35. Leonine lair

37. Bill Clinton's veep

38. Ike's initials

39. Event with bucking broncos

40. Actress MacDowell

42. Beach Boys hit, "___ John B"

44. Baby bovine

46. Hunters' org.

48. Show hosts, for short

50. Ernie on the links

51. Wall St. regulator

52. Capote, to friends

53. Norm: abbr.

Solution on Page 287

ACROSS

1. Do the floor
4. Not a ___ out of you!: "Shh!"
8. Bloke
12. Neighbor of Miss.
13. "It's ___ big mistake!"
14. "Stretch" car
15. With it
16. Swim sans suit
18. Tennis champ Chris
20. ___ off (plenty mad)
21. Send another way
23. Put on hold
27. Apple centers
28. "It ___ far far better thing…"
29. Quieted (down)
31. Went off course
34. Paranormal showman Geller
35. Ken and Barbie
36. "E" on a gas gauge
39. Poor movie rating
42. Jockey's strap
44. Peach ___ (dessert)
45. Upper hand
49. *Monday Night Football* network
50. Tailor's line
51. "Let's call ___ evening"
52. Unidentified John
53. Shoemaker's tools
54. Aug. follower
55. Since 1/1: abbr.

DOWN

1. *Politically Incorrect* host Bill
2. Martini garnish
3. Office fastener
4. Grazing land
5. Lodge member
6. Upper crusts
7. Window unit
8. Bonnie's partner in crime
9. Kept out of sight
10. "___ my brother's keeper?"
11. Mom's mate
17. Homer Simpson's neighbor
19. Kitchen or bath
22. Bill's "excellent adventure" partner
24. Presidential partner
25. WNW's opposite
26. "Groovy!"
29. Billiard stick
30. One of an octopus's octet
31. Germany's Otto ___ Bismarck
32. Gold or silver
33. "What ___ is new?"
35. Present to Goodwill, e.g.
37. Aerial railway cars
38. Tokyo dough

40. Monastery head

41. Sprinted

43. "How sweet ___!"

45. Red ___ beet

46. Morning dampness

47. Kilmer of *At First Sight*

48. Noticeable opening

Solution on Page 287

ACROSS

1. Like Abner
4. Mario who wrote *The Godfather*
8. "Shape up or ___ out!"
12. *ER* setting
13. Not many
14. Listen to
15. Follower of Nov.
16. Took a taxi
17. Military force
18. Place for a blotter
20. Reservoir creator
22. Tibet's Dalai ___
25. Grand Canyon pack animal
29. Nothing, in Mexico
32. "What'll ___?" (bartender's question)
34. Dog days mo.
35. Higher than zero, on an altimeter
38. *Frasier* network
39. "___ in every garage"
40. Hitchhiker's need
41. Desert spring
43. Miniature plateau
45. Dem.'s opponent
47. Letter carriers' org.
50. Go up
53. First part of a play
56. Spruce relative
58. Pen fluids
59. Chimney dirt
60. J. Edgar Hoover's org.
61. Tiny pest
62. "___ Enchanted Evening" (*South Pacific* song)
63. 1/6 fl. oz.

DOWN

1. Cookie jar topper
2. Frosted
3. Clare Boothe ___
4. Cold-weather jacket
5. Area 51 craft, supposedly
6. A's opposite, in England
7. Was in the red
8. SeaWorld whale
9. Woody Allen's *Hannah and ___ Sisters*
10. "___ a Rock": Simon and Garfunkel
11. Ask too many questions
19. Eastern European
21. One slain by Cain
23. Various: abbr.
24. Mr. T series, with *The*
26. Sitar player Shankar
27. Had misgivings about
28. Eye up and down
29. One billionth: prefix
30. "Dancing Queen" pop group
31. Physicians, briefly
33. Not clothed

PUZZLE 119

36. "___ On Down the Road"

37. Cenozoic and Paleozoic

42. "___ my case"

44. High-end hotel option

46. Skip a turn

48. Kaput sound

49. Bro and sis

50. 18-wheeler

51. Country lodge

52. Reggae relative

54. Dove's sound

55. Male turkey

57. Tear (up)

Solution on Page 287

PUZZLES • 249

ACROSS

1. Cries of aversion
5. ___ Zeppelin
8. Not a good way to run
12. Tooth or plant part
13. "Can ___ now?"
14. Toe the ___ (obey)
15. ___ Star State (Texas)
16. Like bass notes
17. Electric cord's end
18. Ambulance worker, for short
20. *Bonanza* brother
21. Former veep Agnew
24. Book before Nehemiah
27. Big coffee holder
28. Stan's slapstick partner
30. "See ___ care!"
33. Pkg. with money due
34. Reluctant (to)
35. The old man
36. *Big Love* airer
37. Bandleader Shaw
38. ___-friendly (environmentally safe)
39. Roller coaster cry
40. Photographer Adams
42. Postpaid encl.
45. Hosp. scan
46. Wheel rod
47. Hoops grp.
49. MIT grad

53. Use a Kindle, say
54. The "N" in NCO
55. ___ Marie Presley
56. Charitable donations
57. Obi-___ Kenobi
58. Male deer

DOWN

1. Dot-com's address
2. Guck or gunk
3. Darlin'
4. Control the wheel
5. Light tune
6. Swelled head
7. Wall Street index, with "the"
8. Omega's opposite
9. *Venus de* ___
10. Responsibility
11. Beer barrels
19. Simoleons
21. "No ___ luck!"
22. "No ___!" ("Easy!")
23. ___-European languages
24. Tickle pink
25. Cylindrical pasta
26. Try again, as a court case
29. Folk wisdom
30. Midmonth date
31. Confront
32. One with adoring fans

39. Garden intruders

41. Nobel physicist Bohr

42. "___ Smile" (Hall & Oates hit)

43. Skating jump

44. Grand ___ home run

45. Educator Horace

47. SSE's opposite

48. Fluffy scarf

50. Annual coll. basketball competition

51. Fed. purchasing group

52. Old cloth

Solution on Page 287

ACROSS

1. Scored 100 on an exam
5. Lobbying org.
8. Kennel cries
12. Singsong syllables
13. Big commotion
14. Guinness or Waugh
15. Elem. school groups
16. Certain retriever, briefly
17. Italian farewell
18. Deflation sound
19. Chow mein additive
20. Where the heart is
21. Tic ___ (mint)
23. "___ the end of my rope!"
25. Stephen King's state
27. Takes too much of, in a way
28. Tourney pass
31. Esoteric
33. Bug barrier
35. June grads: abbr.
36. "Do Ya Think I'm Sexy?" singer Stewart
38. Diminish in intensity
39. Top-rated
40. Great noise
41. Chili con ___
44. "What ___ you getting at?"
46. Faux ___ (blunder)
49. "And giving ___, up the chimney he rose"
50. Historic time span
51. Stir up
52. "Don't look ___!"
53. ___ Tin Tin
54. Allen of *Manhattan Murder Mystery*
55. Puppy bites
56. Alternative to unleaded: abbr.
57. What to do after you "read 'em"

DOWN

1. Mont Blanc site
2. Andrew Lloyd Webber smash
3. Stretchables
4. Prosecutors, briefly
5. Chums
6. Slowly, in music
7. What corn kernels attach to
8. America's Cup entrant
9. Get caught in ___
10. Pod contents
11. Kilt wearer
19. Three-time Wimbledon champ John
20. Fall like Niagara's waters
22. "I'd like to buy ___, Pat"
24. ER workers
25. Pas' mates
26. The "A" in ETA: abbr.
28. Tall skinny guy
29. "The best is ___ to come"

30. U-turn from WSW

32. Very long time

34. Baseball stat

37. Honeybunch

39. Mountains in Chile

41. *Misery* costar James

42. ___-aging cream

43. Rollick or frolic

45. "You ___?" (butler's question)

47. Senate staffer

48. High-five sound

50. Do something wrong

51. Like sushi

Solution on Page 288

ACROSS

1. Comic DeLuise
4. Chinese leader with a *Little Red Book*
7. Boozehound
10. Santa ___ (hot winds)
12. Creative work
13. Actress Irene of *Fame*
14. Countrywide: abbr.
15. Prefix for giving or taking
16. Ewe's offspring
17. "___ no idea!"
19. Earring sites
20. Modifies
23. Univ. dorm overseers
24. Opposite of fronts
25. Like Abe
28. Kipling novel
29. Not many
30. Hosp. areas
32. Boil
35. Crane's cousin
37. Arrived lifeless, briefly
38. New York's ___ Island
39. White as a ghost
42. SeaWorld barker
43. Nut
44. Clinton's instrument
45. Wise ___ owl
49. Neighbor of Cambodia
50. Ogle
51. Mama's boys
52. Coppertone no.
53. "Kilroy ___ here"
54. "Don't ___ fool!"

DOWN

1. Newsman Rather
2. Keep ___ short leash
3. Welcome ___
4. Papas' partners
5. Desertlike
6. Tiebreaking periods, briefly
7. Swedish car
8. *Coffee, Tea ___?*
9. Keep ___ on (watch)
11. More like a fox
13. Neck and neck
18. Mins. and mins.
19. PC linking acronym
20. *Raiders of the Lost ___*
21. Luau necklaces
22. No longer wild
23. Propel a boat
25. Tee-___
26. Separate the laundry
27. Beech or birch
29. Mortgage org.
31. RR depot
33. Perfect places

34. Big weight

35. Inbound flight approx.

36. Black-tie affairs

38. Male and female

39. "___ fair in love and war"

40. Cleansing agent

41. Horseshoe site

42. "Don't ___ word!"

44. Do needlework

46. Weep

47. "Gimme ___!" (end of a Yale cheer)

48. Hush-hush govt. org.

Solution on Page 288

Answers

Puzzle 2

Puzzle 3

Puzzle 4

Puzzle 1

```
S A C S . N A B . M E X
U T A H . L I C E . I B M
D I V E . O P U S . M B A
S T E L L A . R E M I S S
. . . . I N N A T E . .
M P H . Z E E . . A R M S
U S E D . R A M . D I N O
M I N E . . T O W . B O W
. . . A S H O R E . . .
P R O N T O . O D D I T Y
E E K . O W N S . O K I E
N P R . O T H E . D E C A
T O A . L O L . . O A K S
```

Puzzle 5

G	R	E	T	A	■	D	D	S	■	■	E	T	C
U	N	A	R	M	■	P	A	C	■	■	L	O	L
M	A	R	I	O	■	I	M	A	G	I	N	E	
■	■	N	E	R	D	■	E	R	R	A	T	A	■
C	A	E	S	A	R	S	■	C	A	N	O	N	■
O	J	S	■	L	A	N	C	E	S	■	■	■	
N	A	T	S	■	M	O	O	■	P	H	A	T	
■	■	■	T	R	A	U	M	A	■	A	L	L	
I	M	B	U	E	■	T	I	T	A	N	I	C	
T	E	E	N	S	Y	■	C	O	B	S	■	■	
S	T	A	T	I	O	N	■	L	O	O	M	S	
O	R	D	■	S	K	A	■	L	I	L	A	C	
K	O	S	■	T	O	W	■	S	L	O	T	H	

Puzzle 6

O	H	O	H	■	D	A	B	■	A	M	M	O
R	E	N	E	■	A	B	E	■	M	E	U	P
B	E	A	M	■	T	R	E	■	I	N	S	T
E	L	S	■	N	E	O	■	A	S	S	T	S
■	P	I	E	■	A	W	L	S	■	■		
C	A	R	O	B	■	D	E	I	■	C	F	O
A	V	E	N	U	E	■	S	A	L	O	O	N
L	G	E	■	L	A	C	■	S	O	L	E	S
■	■	S	A	R	A	■	E	G	O	■		
C	A	S	T	E	■	B	B	S	■	R	A	P
O	S	A	Y	■	P	A	O	■	G	A	L	A
M	I	N	E	■	A	N	N	■	E	D	E	N
E	A	T	S	■	L	A	G	■	N	O	G	S

Puzzle 7

B	T	U	S	■	O	B	S	■	A	C	A	T
A	A	R	P	■	W	A	T	■	T	E	L	E
D	I	L	L	■	N	N	E	■	W	E	A	N
■	■	A	D	E	E	R	■	A	S	P	S	
S	A	S	S	E	D	■	I	S	R	■		
O	A	T	H	S	■	F	L	A	■	H	A	H
F	A	O	■	E	R	R	E	D	■	I	F	A
T	A	P	■	R	E	I	■	D	A	T	E	S
■	■	A	T	T	■	A	L	L	S	E	T	
P	O	S	T	■	R	O	G	E	T	■		
I	W	A	S	■	A	B	A	■	A	P	I	N
C	I	N	E	■	C	O	P	■	R	A	S	A
S	E	G	A	■	T	E	E	■	S	W	A	B

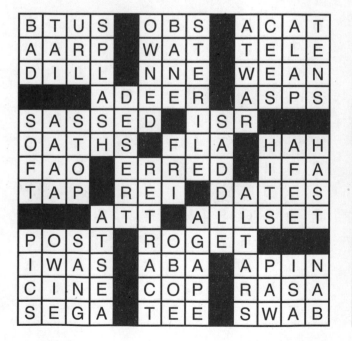

Puzzle 8

B	I	B	■	A	T	N	O	■	S	I	N	G
A	M	I	■	C	R	A	N	■	P	L	E	A
Y	A	K	■	T	Y	N	E	■	E	K	G	S
S	C	E	N	E	■	O	S	H	A	■		
■	■	A	D	D	■	O	R	A	L	B		
S	P	A	T	■	E	B	B	S	■	W	E	E
H	U	N	■	B	E	T	A	S	■	H	O	C
U	S	N	■	E	M	U	S	■	B	O	N	K
T	H	A	I	S	■	S	C	I	■	■		
■	■	N	O	D	S	■	A	O	R	T	A	
E	R	O	S	■	A	I	D	S	■	B	U	S
S	A	K	E	■	B	R	U	T	■	I	S	H
C	Y	S	T	■	S	I	B	S	■	S	K	Y

Puzzle 9

```
V A T   D U M A     P H D
E C G   E N C L   S H O E
G H I   C O A L   C O P Y
  E F O R   T O T O
    F E D   T A U N T
E A S T E R N   B R I A R
N B A   J U G       T K O
D R I L L   T O P S E E D
  A L I A S   V A N
    O V I D   T O M B
M O W N   D A Z E   G E M
I T A S   E V E N   R A G
I C H   B E E T   S U M
```

Puzzle 9

Puzzle 10

```
G T E   S P F     D E N G
O H S   H A D A   E X I T
N Y T   E R R S   L E N O
    I K E A   S W E D E S
L A M A R   M E A T
I C A N   B A R R E L S
B A T   D A N T E   Y O M
  R E S O L E S   D R O P
    M I L S   B E I N G
C A S I N O   B L O C
I G O R   T Y R A   I V Y
T O N K   S E A N   S H U
E G G S     N Y C   T S K
```

Puzzle 10

Puzzle 11

```
A S A   A L T S   E A R P
P O T   B O A T   A M O R
P A T   A N T I   S I L O
T R Y S T   R E E S E S
    S E T   S N L
O P E N S E A   T S A R S
R E P   D A Y   D A R
S T A S H   A T A L O S S
    O O N   D R E
S T E R E O   L A S T S
H O M E   M A Z E   A I L
A R T S   A N I N   P E A
G I S T   D O T E   S A G
```

Puzzle 11

Puzzle 12

```
B A D E   A D M   Q U I T
A T E E   G I T   U N D O
L O B E   R E S T E A S Y
S L R     S T R E W
A L A M O D E   A N A M E
    A T I L T   B R I T
S C H I S M   S P E E D S
I D O L   S T A G E
P E S O S   E R A S E R S
  A R K I N     I O C
H A N D I C A P   F E M A
A C N E   E N C   T I E D
S E A R   S T S   C O O S
```

Puzzle 12

260

Puzzle 13

```
MAR   CAVE  BOGS
IQS   ABIG  AROW
GUT   DONG  KOBE
SAUCER    SENSE
    ATTACH
CHRIS   DOH   KWH
RUIN   JAY   COVE
YEP   WAG  BROAD
     ARETOO
SCALD     ESPRIT
NOLO  LYES   ASK
ILLS  BONE   MNO
PEAT  JOYS   POS
```

Puzzle 14

```
NFL UKE   ALIST
TRU SIX   SUSHI
HOTSEAT   CRIED
   HAD    BEETLE
OVEN  ATEN
HIRE   ROADRACE
MBAS  ENG    ELLY
SENTINEL    GLUE
     RODE   RIBS
STOPIT    DEN
HULAS  LEOTARD
ANGIE  BMW   LOU
HEALS  SUN   LYE
```

Puzzle 15

```
BIL   RPMS   FIT
OPUS  ILET   ASU
YOGA  TADA   TAG
    FIAT  TREKS
BABES   FUSE
UPA  IMOK   BALD
CAR  SORER  NAY
KLEE  AMSO  DIE
    ESTS  SOARS
SMALL   HESA
PAR  ITON   FIRM
AUF  TEED   SOUP
MIS  SASS   UGH
```

Puzzle 16

```
PEI   BUN   SUES
AYN   ROSA  INMY
GED   OUST  FLED
ELICIT   ASTERN
REGAL   LASSIE
  TON  DIT   SLY
    SADDEST
FAR  LIT    HOR
LLAMAS    CARED
ABSENT   ROTATE
VIPS  ANON   TIP
ONEA  NEWS   ONT
RODS  TVS    RAH
```

Puzzle 17

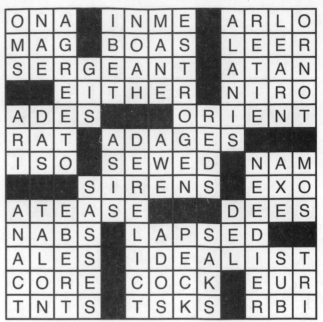

Puzzle 18

Puzzle 19

Puzzle 20

262

Puzzle 21

```
T A N S . . P E G . I N K
I S A S . S A V E . C U E
E W A N . C H I N . O K D
S E N S O R . C R A N E S
. . . . P E S T E R . . .
V E T . T A U . . C O W S
I F W E . M R S . H O P E
I G O T . . G E L . F A X
. . . A S P E C T . . . .
A V A T A R . E R A S E S
F I N . W A R D . L A R K
L S U . E D I E . F U M E
Y E T . D A D . . A L A W
```

Puzzle 22

```
M A I . A F R O . P I T S
E R N . L A O S . R I N G
R D S . B A L L P O I N T
G E O D E . L O E B . . .
E N F O R C E . R E C U R
. . A C T O R . . H M M
W A R S A W . D E M E A N
I N A . . . C O N E S . .
L I S T S . E L A S T I C
. . . H E R R . M A N O R
H A I R P I E C E . U N E
I A T E . P A U L . T I E
C H A W . E L M S . S A D
```

Puzzle 23

```
G P S . C A N E . T O S S
U S E . A R O N . A L I E
T S E . R I D S . C E N T
S T A P L E . N O I S E S
. . . A A S . A R T . . .
A B A T . P R E . A D E
M A P S . A T E . A P E D
T A R . L T S . C O T S
. . M I T . S A T . . .
T A M A L E . I N S E A M
H U E S . S O R T . A G A
I D E S . T R E E . T E N
S I T E . S A N D . A S I
```

Puzzle 24

```
L A M A . B I T . . K I D
A C A N . A C H . I N S O
L I L O . N Y E . S O L O
A D L I B S . S Y S T E M
. . . N A H . E D U . . .
O A K T R E E . S E R I F
Z S A . . E L F . . C C I
S P I E D . M I S T A K E
. . . P U P . N P R . . .
M E M O I R . A R O M A S
A M E X . O M G . P A T H
A I R Y . N I L . I T O O
M T V . G R E . C A M P
```

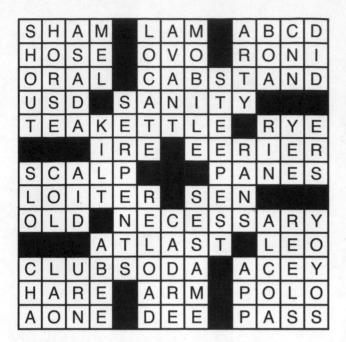

Puzzle 25

Puzzle 26

Puzzle 27

Puzzle 28

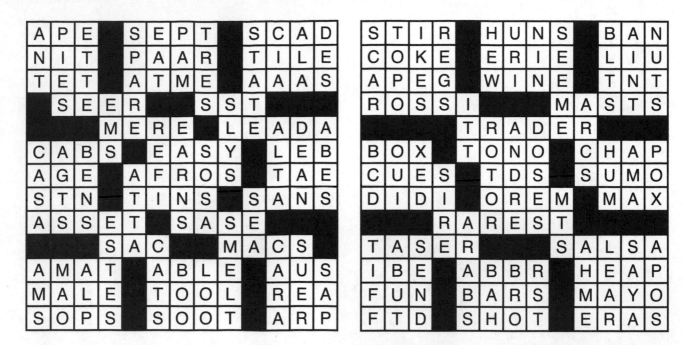

Puzzle 29

Puzzle 30

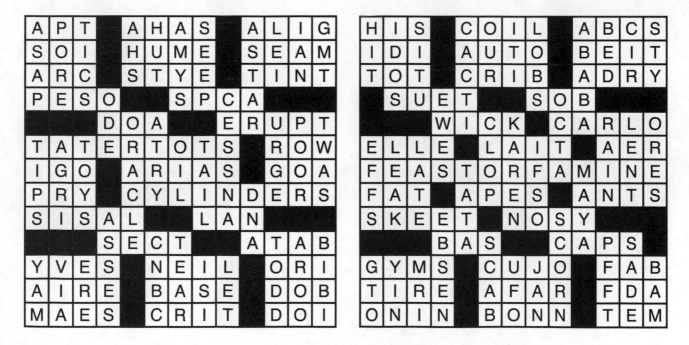

Puzzle 31

Puzzle 32

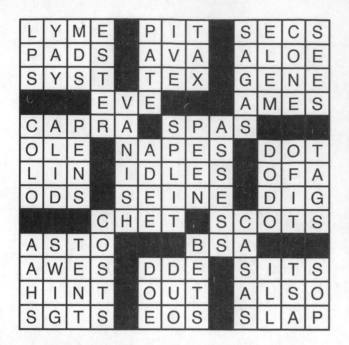

Puzzle 33

```
L Y M E . P I T . S E C S
P A D S . A V A . A L O E
S Y S T . T E X . G E N E
. . E V E . . . A M E S .
C A P R A . S P A S . . .
O L E . N A P E S . D O T
L I N . I D L E S . O F A
O D S . S E I N E . D I G
. . C H E T . S C O T S .
A S T O . . B S A . . . .
A W E S . D D E . S I T S
H I N T . O U T . A L S O
S G T S . E O S . S L A P
```

Puzzle 34

```
P L A T . C S I . M E S O
R I L E . A H H . O P E N
O M E N . B E A . M I S C
F A C E C A R D S . S S E
. . . T A R P . T R O I .
P S A . N E A . E N D O W
E A T S A T . R E S E N T
E L L I S . P E P . S S S
. T A C T . I D L E . . .
S I N . A G R E E A B L E
U N T O . L A Y . R O A M
L E I A . I T E . L O V E
U S S R . B E S . S P A R
```

Puzzle 35

```
T A O . A M P S . T H A W
A R F . B E R T . A M B I
J I M . L I A R . V O U S
. D E L A . Y U L E . . .
. . U Z I . T E R R O R .
D E S C E N T . S N O R E
E L K . B I D . . B B C .
M E E T S . C O N T E S T
S E E R E D . M E W . . .
. . I C E D . A A N D . .
F O R K . R O O T . Y A P
L A K E . M U S E . P L O
U F O S . A R U N . D E P
```

Puzzle 36

```
K I N . M A N S . A M I N
O O O . A C E S . C O S A
I N S . P H E W . L E A P
. S E A L E D . O U S T S
. . L E S S E R . . . . .
A B E T . . . S E T T E R
N O M A D S . E L A I N E
E N T R E E . . K N E W .
. . . A E R A T E . . . .
B A B A R . A L A S K A .
A C O P . A D I P . A M P
A U R A . H A V E . M E A
S T A T . A R E S . A N D
```

Puzzle 37

```
MOP   ASKS  AFR
ANAS  CULT  RIO
SOSO  ONME  ALT
  LAWS  ANTES
SABER  HAMS
ATO  UTIL  ALBA
GIN  TANKS  AIM
SEAT  REAL  COO
  OATS  ABYSS
CASES  TAME
ALE  SNAG  SSSS
RAN  NOTE  SPAY
SIS  SPED  YON
```

Puzzle 38

```
IFI  ASIF  SLUM
PIN  RENO  TONE
ACAPULCO  RICH
DANUBE  TWOS
  NACL  INLAW
PTAS  TAILGATE
AWL  TESTY  NOV
RIPTIDES  PEPE
SNARL  RALE
  CALL  DOLLAR
CHIC  OVERTURE
AUNT  MEAN  CEL
BROS  BELA  KAY
```

Puzzle 39

```
DAH  FCC  TOWN
IMY  ALPS  ASHE
RED  VERT  CHOW
TREMOR  AOK
  IRK  TOSSED
BRASS  DIM  TGI
AILS  DEC  BEAN
GOT  XER  SANDS
STOKES  FIR
  ISP  AERIAL
HUGO  OLIN  THU
EARS  TORN  CII
EWOK  YEA  HTS
```

Puzzle 40

```
IWO  ASH  AIMAT
SON  LTD  SNAFU
OVA  BALDEAGLE
FENDER  ITIN
  ORRIN  REBA
SLANTED  SOD
EURO  DIA  GIRD
INE  ORLEANS
SAAB  UTTER
  CRAM  DRILLS
GROOMSMEN  EAU
AUDIT  ICE  CCC
PEELS  NOR  HEH
```

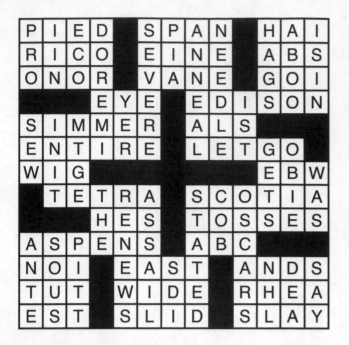

Puzzle 41

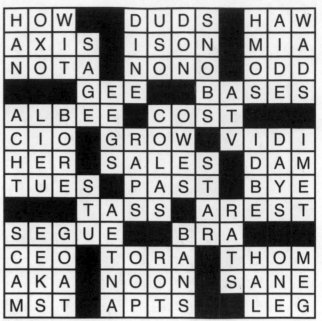

Puzzle 42

Puzzle 43

Puzzle 44

Puzzle 45

H	A	L	L		S	H	A		S	O	P	H
O	H	I	O		L	E	N		C	R	U	E
E	O	N	S		A	F	T		A	B	B	Y
S	T	E	E	L	S		L	O	T			
			S	H	R	E	W		M	A	J	
A	W	A	R	D		O	R	E	G	A	N	O
M	I	T	E		K	G	S		P	I	N	A
A	N	E	M	O	N	E		R	A	M	E	N
N	O	M		W	O	R	S	E				
	W	N	W		T	O	A	S	T	S		
F	A	Y	E		H	B	O		L	E	E	K
I	M	A	S		O	R	R		O	M	N	I
G	Y	N	T		W	R	Y		G	I	N	S

Puzzle 46

M	O	N	O		P	V	C		S	W	A	G
I	R	O	N		O	O	H		E	A	R	N
S	E	E	K		T	W	I		A	N	K	A
T	O	L	E	D	O		L	O	W	E	S	T
		Y	U	M		D	Y	E				
P	B	S		D	A	N		L	E	N	D	S
S	I	A	M		C	B	S		D	I	R	E
I	N	L	A	Y		C	T	R		X	Y	Z
	L	O	B		R	U	T					
S	T	P	A	U	L		O	M	E	G	A	S
P	O	L	I		U	S	B		M	A	G	I
E	G	O	S		S	U	E		P	L	U	G
W	A	D	E		H	R	S		T	E	E	N

Puzzle 47

O	I	L	E	R		B	I	N		E	S	S
A	N	I	M	E		I	S	A		A	L	T
T	E	L	E	P	A	T	H	Y		R	A	E
	R	S	T		S	A	N	T	A			
T	R	I	G		O	F	A		N	E	E	D
A	B	N	E	R		A	M	E	N	S		
P	I	T		A	L	L	I	N		T	A	G
	H	A	D	E	S		T	I	L	D	E	
T	O	E	S		D	E	A		N	Y	S	E
A	P	L	U	S		C	O	D				
L	E	O		L	A	S	T	D	I	T	C	H
C	R	O		O	N	A		D	R	I	V	E
S	A	P		P	A	W		S	A	S	S	Y

Puzzle 48

P	A	S	T	A		N	A	P		M	I	D
U	P	P	E	R		Y	U	L		E	D	U
P	R	I	S	M		T	R	A	I	N	E	E
	K	H	A	N		A	N	N	U	A	L	
C	E	E		N	O	O	S	E	S			
R	A	L	E	I	G	H		T	O	P	I	C
A	C	E	D		O	A	R		L	E	N	A
T	H	E	I	R		R	E	S	E	A	L	S
	T	O	M	A	T	O		R	A	H		
A	N	Y	O	N	E		D	U	C	T		
D	I	O	R	A	M	A		R	A	R	E	R
A	N	G		L	O	L		E	M	E	R	Y
M	A	I		D	S	L		D	E	E	R	E

Puzzle 49

```
P U B ■ P A D ■ ■ A I M S
E P A ■ O N U P ■ C O A T
D I R T P O O R ■ M U S S
I N N E E D ■ A R E ■ ■ ■
■ ■ ■ L Y E ■ I N S A N E
S M I L E ■ S S S ■ M I X
L O S S ■ P O E ■ P A C E
U R N ■ L O T ■ A I D E S
G E T S E T ■ I S T ■ ■ ■
■ ■ T A E ■ S T A B L E
O T H E ■ N O A H S A R K
R E A P ■ T R A M ■ J O E
D A N S ■ ■ R C A ■ A N D
```

Puzzle 50

```
D U P E ■ C H A ■ ■ M T S
A D I N ■ D E G ■ M A U L
T O N S ■ S S N ■ O C T O
A N G U S ■ E R N E S T
■ ■ ■ R P M ■ W E E ■ ■
U S H E R E D ■ A T R E E
S K A ■ D O M ■ ■ O W N
S I T E S ■ A E R A T E D
■ ■ ■ L O S ■ H A L ■ ■
M A R I N E ■ ■ P E T I T
I T I S ■ C H E ■ R O S H
L O G E ■ T A B ■ T I M E
L B S ■ ■ S I B ■ S T E M
```

Puzzle 49   **Puzzle 50**

Puzzle 51

```
O T S ■ A F E W ■ R A P T
C O T ■ N I N O ■ A L L Y
T V A ■ D E V O ■ V I A L
■ ■ R V S ■ F L E E C E
A C T I O N S ■ A S N E R
B A L M ■ A N O X ■ ■ ■
C D E ■ N A W ■ T O Z
■ ■ C U R E ■ M O D E
H E L L O ■ E N G A R D E
A V A I L S ■ H O P ■
D I B S ■ O H N O ■ E F G
T T O P ■ L O U S ■ D E P
O A R S ■ D I N T ■ O Z S
```

Puzzle 52

```
■ S P A W N ■ S U S A N ■
S T E V I E ■ A S Y L U M
C R E A S E ■ V E N I C E
A I R ■ E D G E S ■ E L O
R V E R ■ L A S ■ ■ N E W
S E D A T E S ■ B A S I S
■ ■ ■ K O S ■ R I D ■ ■
S A F E S ■ R E C I T A L
T S E ■ G E M ■ M E T A
O L D ■ D R O O P ■ N O N
P E O R I A ■ R E F U N D
S E R I E S ■ S N A R E S
■ P A N T S ■ E N D E D ■
```

Puzzle 51   **Puzzle 52**

270

Puzzle 53

O	P	T			A	N	D	I			F	L	E	W
F	O	R			C	Y	A	N			R	A	V	I
F	L	U			T	E	D	S			E	Y	E	R
S	E	E	N	O				M	E	S	S	Y		
			E	N	C	A	S	E						
B	O	M	B			R	U	N	T			M	P	H
B	U	D			I	O	T	A	S			B	I	O
Q	T	S			T	O	O	K			B	A	N	G
				U	N	S	E	A	T					
C	L	A	M	P					L	U	R	I	D	
R	U	D	E			R	A	Z	E			E	M	U
A	L	O	W			E	X	E	C			A	N	S
B	U	G	S			D	E	N	S			M	O	T

Puzzle 54

P	L	U	S			P	B	S			F	L	U	B
J	A	N	E			O	L	E			L	O	R	E
S	P	O	T			R	U	N			I	W	I	N
			T	Y	K	E		C	R	E	S	T		
C	H	I	L	E			I	N	A	T				
M	E	T	E	S			N	O	T			I	N	D
O	M	S			L	T	D					T	A	O
N	S	A			B	A	H			S	E	L	M	A
			T	A	T	E			A	X	L	E	S	
C	O	D	E	S			F	A	D	E				
A	V	O	N			M	A	P			M	O	L	T
R	A	G	S			E	C	O			P	O	O	H
E	L	S	E			W	E	D			T	O	G	O

Puzzle 55

T	A	F	T			A	Y	N			S	H	O	W
U	B	E	R			M	O	E			T	E	R	I
R	O	T	E			P	R	O	V	E	R	B	S	
K	W	A	N			K	N	O	W					
			D	U	G			L	E	D	G	E		
L	I	L	Y	P	A	D			D	A	N	G		
A	T	M			S	P	U	R	T			M	U	G
P	A	N	T			D	E	B	U	S	S	Y		
S	L	O	S	H				V	A	N				
			H	I	F	I			C	H	E	X		
A	C	C	I	D	E	N	T			L	A	M	B	
P	O	U	R			S	N	O			E	L	M	O
B	O	L	T			S	O	W			S	T	Y	X

Puzzle 56

F	A	A			S	T	E	P			B	O	D	E
A	B	S			H	U	L	A			A	W	O	L
C	U	P			A	B	A	D			C	L	E	F
E	S	C					T	R	E	K				
T	E	A	L			P	E	E	L			L	I	B
			I	R	A	S			L	E	A	V	E	
D	I	N	N	E	R		D	E	E	M	E	D		
E	D	I	T	S			C	O	N	N				
C	O	B			E	A	R	L			Y	A	D	A
			C	E	D	E					F	I	R	
O	F	F	A			O	O	H	S			L	A	D
N	O	E	S			P	L	I	E			A	N	O
S	O	B	S			T	E	M	P			C	A	R

Puzzle 57

```
M I N I ▪ ▪ R N A ▪ J A M
O F A N ▪ S O I L ▪ O J S
W A N T ▪ T Y P O ▪ S A G
S T A L E R ▪ A N G E R S
▪ ▪ ▪ N E S T E A ▪ ▪ ▪
W R Y ▪ G E T ▪ R A M S
O U T A ▪ T O E ▪ B L A H
W E D S ▪ L S D ▪ P R Y
▪ ▪ T E R E S A ▪ ▪
A D M I R E ▪ A S S I S T
L O A ▪ O N L Y ▪ C A P O
L T S ▪ D E U S ▪ A M I D
S H H ▪ E E G ▪ N A T O
```

Puzzle 58

```
B S A ▪ S P E L L ▪ M E L
I T S ▪ A R T O O ▪ A Y E
D O C ▪ N O H I T ▪ N E T
E M I R ▪ T E N S E D ▪
S P I E G E L ▪ R A S H
▪ ▪ H I S ▪ D I E T E R
A S S E R T ▪ E M C E E S
S T E A L S ▪ C U T ▪
P A C T ▪ A R S E N A L
▪ U S A B L E ▪ D O R A
S I R ▪ P A G A N ▪ W I T
O N E ▪ O B E S E ▪ A S I
P C S ▪ P A R E D ▪ Y E N
```

Puzzle 59

```
D I O N ▪ B A L E ▪ D J S
E G G O ▪ O W E D ▪ A O L
G E R M ▪ A L M S ▪ I K E
S T E E P ▪ E A S E D
▪ ▪ S T A L L S ▪
F C C ▪ T O M Y ▪ O H M Y
A I R S ▪ N P R ▪ F E A R
N A T L ▪ G L E E ▪ W T S
▪ O B S E S S ▪
B A D G E ▪ T H U M B
A P U ▪ F I N D ▪ T H R U
B O D ▪ I S E E ▪ T O E D
E X E ▪ T R O Y ▪ P H D S
```

Puzzle 60

```
G O O ▪ F U R L ▪ T H U G
I N N ▪ O F U S ▪ H E L L
G T E ▪ R O M A ▪ I N C A
▪ H I T ▪ T I E R E D
I N A S E C ▪ A F I R E
F I L M ▪ A T T N ▪
S P F ▪ F O E ▪ R O D
▪ P E T A ▪ C A T O
L E T M E ▪ S T I T C H
E R R A N T ▪ I D A ▪
V I I I ▪ A S I N ▪ T W I
E C O L ▪ P A R E ▪ A H S
L A S S ▪ E L K S ▪ T O P
```

272

SPIN RAYS INK
LIME OBIT SUE
YEAS MYNA TNN
THEE GROSS
PHASE ASA
RAS AFIT GAWK
ELK ROAMS GER
SEAL IMSO URI
ESE RATES
BABEL AHEM
OSU ALVA ISMS
POR BOOT SLIT
SNL SOWS HOLD

Puzzle 61

SNAIL DIE ENE
HENNA EON DEE
EXALT ANI HEE
STPETER GPA
TEAM MERLE
UKE GETAGRIP
SANDAL ASSISI
ETHEREAL SAC
ROAST DIAS
NIL RAREBIT
TAC ENO ODETO
ORE SRI SALON
MIS SAT ENTRY

Puzzle 62

MUMS AWED TAT
OPEC NOVA ODS
PAIR TEARDROP
STRIPE NEET
MONA LOAF
SUSPEND ALIKE
ICH TAMES SIS
FLOSS EMINENT
TAWT NUDE
CURB LETHAL
ALANALDA TERA
DOS SUIT LAUD
DUE PETE EDGY

Puzzle 63

SHIN RDS BONO
KARO ADE ARAB
ITAT TEE BAHS
DENSE DRS
LAPSE MOW
SHASTA FARCE
CEOS TRA BITS
ALOHA STRESS
BLT AREAR
BAA SCRAM
PAGE STL HOPI
AVIS PIA EVEL
SENT SEW MEND

Puzzle 64

Puzzle 65

```
I F F Y | . | T I P | . | S W I M
C L U E | . | U S C | . | T E N O
K O N A | . | B U T | . | R E D O
. | S W A P | . | R A D O N
P I N T A | . | . | J E T | .
A W A S H | . | L I L A C S
M O P | . | P I G | . | L I P
. | N E S T E D | . | L E O N E
. | N O W | . | A N G S T
M C C O Y | . | S U B S | .
O A H U | . | U M S | . | I S P Y
S L A T | . | M U D | . | G H I A
H E R S | . | P G A | . | N E C K
```

Puzzle 66

```
F U R S | . | I G O | . | I N K Y
I N O N | . | L O N | . | D A N A
R I T E | . | L P S | . | E R I K
E X H A L E | . | E N A C T S
. | D O G | . | T I M | .
D R Y | . | B A D | . | H A N G S
D I E S | . | L I E | . | N O R A
T O T E M | . | P M S | . | S E X
. | N T H | . | B I D | .
E N D I V E | . | A T O D D S
N E R O | . | N H L | . | L O E W
T H U R | . | C U M | . | E Z R A
R I M S | . | E M S | . | D E N Y
```

Puzzle 67

```
N A G S | . | P A C | . | P R I M
A L L I | . | A R R | . | L E V I
I P O D | . | T O A | . | O P E R
R O W E | . | H U T | . | D O S E
. | B A S S E T S | .
R A W E R | . | E R A | . | M R I
E L I T E | . | S T O U T
T I N | . | A R F | . | T A N G O
. | A L E R T E D | .
W O W S | . | C E O | . | P A L O
A M A P | . | A S K | . | O V E R
R A C E | . | N N E | . | L I N G
T R O N | . | T O N | . | E D D Y
```

Puzzle 68

```
F I G | . | I B M | . | D O G G
U Z I | . | G U S T | . | R U M S
J O G | . | E R G O | . | O R C A
I D I O T S | . | P L O | .
. | K I T | . | H E L P E D
S T P A T | . | B A N | . | L A Y
A W A Y | . | P U T | . | F A V A
G I L | . | C O N | . | L I N E N
A T M O S T | . | M O D | .
. | I I I | . | A N E M I C
A G U N | . | O R M E | . | D N A
F L A K | . | N E E R | . | S U N
T O W S | . | P T S | . | E P I
```

274

Puzzle 69

```
T O Y A   L M N   A B O X
L O O N   Y E A   C A K E
C H U G   R I B   C H E R
      O X E N   M E N D S
W H A L E       B O S
N O V A S   G O S S I P
W W I     B I G     P O D
  E V A D E S   R A S P Y
  V I A     A N O S E
I D T A G   B M W S
F O U L   W O O   W I S H
I T N O   S L R   E Q U I
M O A N   W O N   R S V P
```

Puzzle 70

```
R A F   S I C S   E G G
E B A Y   T O U T   P E A
V E R A   P U R R   L A V
S L A N G   S T A T U R E
  W K R P     Y E R
C P A   A H A B   L I K E
C R Y   S I N U S   B A T
C O P A   L Y L E   U N S
  L I T     L A B S
R O A M I N G   S A U D I
U P C   L A I D   S N I T
B E E   T I V O   H U N T
Y D S   S L E W   M O O
```

Puzzle 71

```
A G A I N   P O W   S E R
A N I S E   S E A   O N O
H U L A S K I R T   A D A
      I T A   T A P E D
U R S A   T H U   H O R S
S O P H S   A S C A P
A W E   C O R E A   E A R
  A D I O S   N O R M A
D I K E   P H D   R A C Y
E N E M Y   I F I
E T A   A B A N D O N E D
M R S   R O M   I L I A D
S O Y   D O T   C E N T S
```

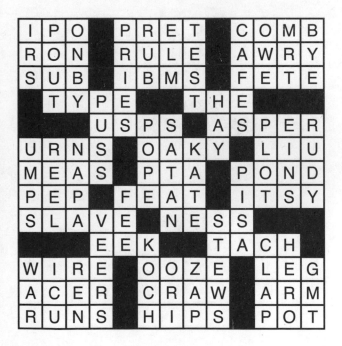

Puzzle 72

```
I P O   P R E T   C O M B
R O N   R U L E   A W R Y
S U B   I B M S   F E T E
  T Y P E     T H E
    U S P S   A S P E R
U R N S   O A K Y   L I U
M E A S   P T A   P O N D
P E P   F E A T   I T S Y
S L A V E   N E S S
    E E K     T A C H
W I R E   O O Z E   L E G
A C E R   C R A W   A R M
R U N S   H I P S   P O T
```

Puzzle 73

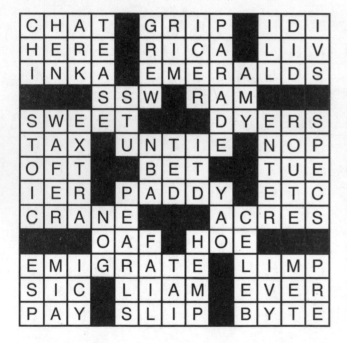

```
N I T . A P P . . D I A N
A T E . T O A D . E T S Y
G E M S T O N E . C A A N
. . O Y L . S K I N N Y .
A L A N S . W I N D . . .
B U N S . C A R E E N S .
A G E . M E L E E . E I N
. S T R A N D S . B A M A
. . I N T O . A E R I E .
E V O N N E . D R E . . .
K I T S . R H E O S T A T
E L I E . S E E M . A P E
S A C S . . F D A . S T N
```

Puzzle 73

Puzzle 74

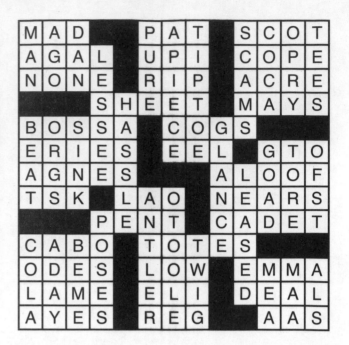

```
M A D . . P A T . S C O T
A G A L . U P I . C O P E
N O N E . R I P . A C R E
. . . S H E E T . M A Y S
B O S S A . C O G S . . .
E R I E S . E E L . G T O
A G N E S . . A L O O F .
T S K . L A O . N E A R S
. . P E N T . C A D E T .
C A B O . T O T E S . . .
O D E S . L O W . E M M A
L A M E . E L I . D E A L
A Y E S . R E G . . A A S
```

Puzzle 74

Puzzle 75

```
C H A T . G R I P . I D I
H E R E . R I C A . L I V
I N K A . E M E R A L D S
. . S S W . R A M . . .
S W E E T . . D Y E R S
T A X . U N T I E . N O P
O F T . B E T . T U E .
I E R . P A D D Y . E T C
C R A N E . A C R E S .
. . O A F . H O E . . .
E M I G R A T E . L I M P
S I C . L I A M . E V E R
P A Y . S L I P . B Y T E
```

Puzzle 75

Puzzle 76

```
S P I C . J D S . C H O P
C O M O . R A N . I O W A
U N I T . S D I . N E L L
D E N T S . S P E N D S .
. . A P O . E V A . . .
N I A G A R A . E M A I L
A C M E . S S T . O L D E
T E A C H . S A D N E S S
. . H O T . N O R . . .
. L E E R E D . N O N O S
B I D E . R E S . L O F T
U Z I S . M F A . L U N E
M A T E . S T Y . S N O W
```

Puzzle 76

Puzzle 77

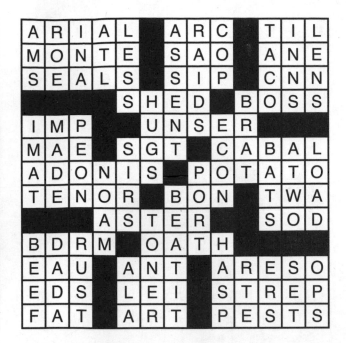

```
H O L A · I F I T · O F F
A X E L · R U B E · F R I
W O O L · K E E N · L A G
· N O V E L · S E A T S
E L A T E D · B E G · ·
M O R S E · A B S O R B
T A D · M I C · E U R
· N O T B A D · P R A N K
· D A Y · S E E S T O
B L A S T · H A R M S ·
L O P · O R E G · O U T S
U N I · N O D E · T R A P
R I G · S O Y S · E E R Y
```

Puzzle 78

```
A R I A L · A R C · T I L
M O N T E · S A O · A N E
S E A L S · S I P · C N N
· S H E D · B O S S
I M P · U N S E R · ·
M A E · S G T · C A B A L
A D O N I S · P O T A T O
T E N O R · B O N · T W A
· A S T E R · S O D
B D R M · O A T H · ·
E A U · A N T · A R E S O
E D S · L E I · S T R E P
F A T · A R T · P E S T S
```

Puzzle 79

```
H U M S · C B S · L I M B
A S N O · H A S · O N E I
G O O N · I R E · C O M A
· A D A B · P A R E S
W R O T E · E V I L · ·
H O G A N · C A P E C O D
E S L · T U T · O D E
E Y E S O R E · M A R I E
· T H U S · O L D E R
C D R O M · A L M A · ·
U R A L · D U I · M A D D
P A N E · A C E · O K I E
S T A N · M E N · S A M S
```

Puzzle 80

```
B A I O · S C H · B B Q S
I M O N · H U E · R E E K
N O W I · A E R · I N D Y
S K E T C H · A U G · ·
· P S A L M · T K O
I D L E R · I D A H O A N
S O A K · S R S · M U T T
A N N E T T E · T O R S O
N E A · R A D I O · ·
· D I S · R O B O T S
F I F E · H B O · O K R A
I R I S · E R N · B L E W
T A N K · S O S · S A Y S
```

Puzzle 81

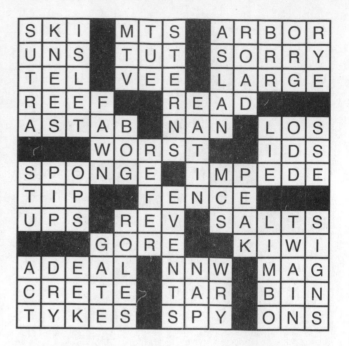

```
R A E   C A L F     L U B E
E R S   O W E R     I B E G
D I S   C L I O     B O R G
    E N O     M O R A L E
M A N I A C     R A T E D
I N C H   O U R S
T S E     E S E     P C S
      C D E F   M A R S
S P E N D     S T A R T S
H A R A S S       E E E
I T E M     I T H E   N S A
R I C E   L E A N   T A N
T O T S   L A D S   S T Y
```

Puzzle 81

Puzzle 82

```
S K I   M T S     A R B O R
U N S   T U T     S O R R Y
T E L   V E E     L A R G E
R E E F     R E A D
A S T A B   N A N     L O S
    W O R S T       I D S
S P O N G E   I M P E D E
T I P     F E N C E
U P S   R E V   S A L T S
    G O R E     K I W I
A D E A L   N N W   M A G
C R E T E   T A R   B I N
T Y K E S   S P Y   O N S
```

Puzzle 82

Puzzle 83

```
N O S   R A P     W A V Y
I N K   P R E   L O U I E
B A A   M A T   S E G E R
S I T     B E A D
  R E F   I S M   N A G
    R C A   C A B A L A
L U G E S     R A M P S
E R O T I C   O F T
S N O   P I C   H A S
    F A S T   D O S
S C O P E   L O G   D U E
O O H E D   A P P   U S C
P O M P   M I S   P A Y
```

Puzzle 83

Puzzle 84

```
G R R   I L L     P O E T
W O O   N I P S   L I V E
E S T   M A S C   A L E X
N E C T A R   R A N
    E T S   A R E T H A
T H R E E   A P R   H E R
R O O M   U K E   D I A M
I M A   R N A   M A N L Y
M O R S E L   G E R
    T O O   E A T I N G
W I F E   C R E D   D A D
S P U N   K E N O   I D A
W O N T   C A W   G A Y
```

Puzzle 84

278

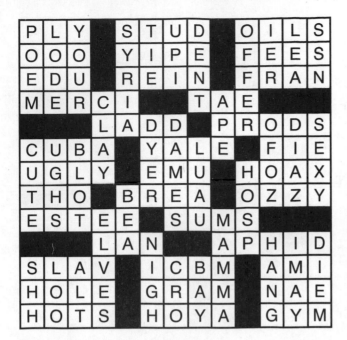

Puzzle 85

Puzzle 86

Puzzle 87

Puzzle 88

Puzzle 89

```
T W A . P J S . I C H
F O I L A A A S L U R
B O L D S K Y R A T A
I N T E N S E R A N T S
. R A W L E E
A T M H O M E A L O N E
N A S A R E X I N O W
D O G P A D D L E A D E
P M S U R I
O G L E S S T A T U T E
F L E A O O H S P U D
F O G S D U O M O B S
M O E E R R E N E
```

Puzzle 90

```
S E A A S K S Y N C
I N N C H I C I A O
D O N C A L C O N Y X
E L U D E N E A T
S A L A D A T T I R E
R E P O S E F I B
H E C K A L E G I B B
I S H P R E S T O
S L E D G E R E I N S
W A N D A R N I E
C A G E T E R N G T E
B I T E P A C O R D
S L O B T H E T O Y
```

Puzzle 91

```
T A G F H A S T A F F
R K O L O L H I N D U
A I D O W L E D G A R
P R O V I D L Y
S A T I N E E L S U P
C O A S T U M S
I G N I T E A C C E P T
F L A I S T O O
S O B S O N B L E S S
F L U E D I C T
C U R I E E L K G R E
O Z O N E Z E E H E N
T I B E T E G G T W O
```

Puzzle 92

```
C H A T R A M G M
B O O B A I R I L A Y
R O P E C D C R U S E
A T S T A K E W A T T S
S O L H I C
B T U L E M O N L A W S
M A R E B E N E L E C
W I L L P O W E R A S H
L A X Y E T
A N V I L A M P E R E S
L E E S H B O R A N T
S I N O R O O S U D S
N I N S Y N E L O
```

Puzzle 93

Puzzle 94

Puzzle 95

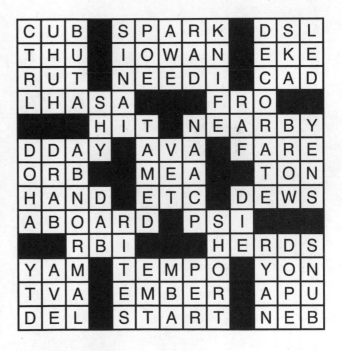

Puzzle 96

Puzzle 97

```
A B C   D D S     T H Y
R Y E S   O U T   C H O O
K E E P   D O A   L A N K
      L O G S   S I N G E
I N T A K E   M I N
S O R T S   R A R E L Y
T W I   S U N     I O N
  S P A R S E   M A D R E
    G I T   S E N S E D
I D L E D   F E L T
C O I N   N U T   I M A X
K E P T   B R O   C A T E
Y R S     A Y N     I T S
```

Puzzle 97

Puzzle 98

```
C V S   R E C D   W H I P
L O W   O I L Y   H A R T
I T A   S N A K E E Y E S
P E T R I   W E A R
    R E T     G E T I T
W H Y S   H I D E   U S O
H U E   S A V O R   T A P
A L L   P I E R   G U Y S
T U L S A     Y E A
    W R A P   A L B U M
S E M E S T E R S   U N O
P L O P   O L A Y   R I O
F I S T   Z E T A   P V T
```

Puzzle 98

Puzzle 99

```
M E T   E P I     S L O W
A G O   N A N S   O I N K
P O P   D I C E   R U T S
    S H U N   A F T
  G E E R   I S A A C S
U N C L E   V O N   L A B
F A R M   F I N   P A L E
O W E   D R E   S E R V E
  S T A Y E D   M A K E
    D E E   P E R K
C H A D   S O U L   E S S
N O P E   T A L L   N E A
N E B R   F L Y   T N N
```

Puzzle 99

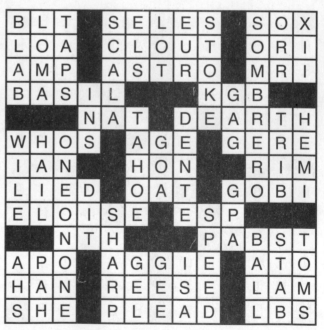

Puzzle 100

```
B L T   S E L E S   S O X
L O A   C L O U T   O R I
A M P   A S T R O   M R I
B A S I L     K G B
    N A T   D E A R T H
W H O S   A G E   G E R E
I A N   H O N   R I M
L I E D   O A T   G O B I
E L O I S E   E S P
    N T H   P A B S T
A P O   A G G I E   A T O
H A N   R E E S E   L A M
S H E   P L E A D   L B S
```

Puzzle 100

Puzzle 101

```
F A A . C E O . . J O G S
I S P . A N N . R A T I O
S I P . T A C . S I S S Y
H A L . . B U S T .
. N E W . L E T . C U P
. . A B E . D E B A S E
J U L I A . . V E R S A
A G A T H A . C A N .
W H Y . M A R . D R S
. . F A C E . O P T
T E M P E . R A M . M I R
E X I L E . I T O . P E I
D E C O . D E W . S L O
```

Puzzle 102

```
L T S . U M A . . C C C
T E A K . S I S . S L A B
D E L I . A N I . P O S E
. L I F T . E A T E R
S P R I G . C I R C
A L A M O . O R N E R Y
M E G A . D N A . N U M B
. D E N T E D . P E S C I
. J I M I . R E H A B
I T W A S . T R O D
T H O R . M I A . L A S H
Z E R O . N O V . E X A M
A N E . O N E . E C O
```

Puzzle 103

```
C P R . S W A M . M E T E
H A I . C O L I . O A K S
I R S . U N U M . C R O C
S T E E L . M E S H
. O L D . P A N G S
P A W N . R A G U . A A H
O F A . I N T E R . T R I
K O S . T O L L . D E P P
E X I S T . S A D
. E Y E D . R E D I D
M I L E . N I K E . O N O
R O O K . V E I N . N F L
T U B S . Y U M A . T O T
```

Puzzle 104

```
O B S . A D J . D R E G
N I P . C O O P . H O L E
O T C . T I N A . A M F M
R E A S O N . N P R
. E N G . D E M O T E
S L A T E S . A W A K E N
T A S . . L A D
A N K A R A . A N N A L S
N E A R E D . R E B
. I N D . R E C E S S
D E G S . I D I D . N I T
E E E E . S A V E . C R Y
S G T S . H E D . L E X
```

Puzzle 105

Puzzle 106

Puzzle 107

Puzzle 108

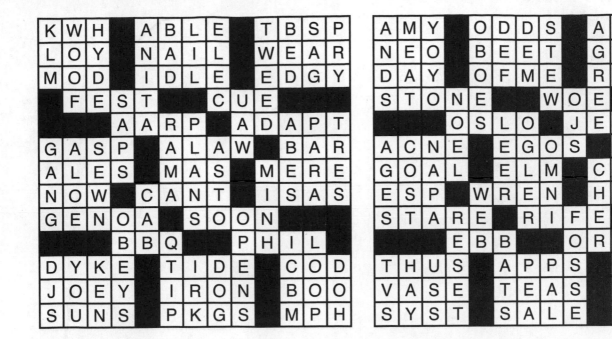

Puzzle 109

Puzzle 110

Puzzle 111

Puzzle 112

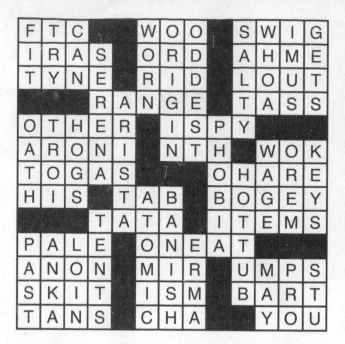

Puzzle 113

Puzzle 114

Puzzle 115

Puzzle 116